"You Better Work!"

MUSIC / CULTURE

A series from Wesleyan University Press

Edited by George Lipsitz, Susan McClary, and Robert Walser

KAI FIKENTSCHER

"You Better Work!"

UNDERGROUND DANCE MUSIC

IN NEW YORK CITY

WESLEYAN UNIVERSITY PRESS

Published by University Press of New England

Hanover & London

Wesleyan University Press

Published by University Press of New England, Hanover, NH 03755

© 2000 by Wesleyan University Press

Printed in United States of America

5 4 3 2 1

CIP data appear at the end of the book

This book was supported by a publication subvention award
from the Society for American Music

Contents

★

Side A

Side B

Illustrations

✦

Preface

The Donkey Show, Disco Bloodbath, Saturday Night Fever—the Musical, The Last Days of Disco, . . . the list of recent products referencing disco goes on. After having been silenced for nearly twenty years, disco music and the culture it spawned seem to be en vogue again, at least to a degree. While the work on this book neared completion, media reports suggested that disco had made a sort of comeback as the "latest prize in the scavenger hunt of the Nostalgia '90s,"[1] a hunt that has treated disco as little more than a curious and bygone phase of American popular culture. Based on the recent commodities (shows, books, and films, even fashions) associated with disco, this conclusion seems reasonably apropos.

However, whereas disco, once scandalous and controversial, may now be deemed safe enough for Broadway revivals and bookstore chains, the spoils of the ongoing hunt so far contain more disco fiction than disco history—as was the case with the original *Saturday Night Fever*. Disco fiction, parading as disco history, has also appeared on TV, at times blending to give us disco, the myth. Those Broadway audiences, who will watch a mock–John Travolta gyrate onstage, may already have read one of the recently published books on Studio 54. Or they may have seen one of the "documentary" programs on cable television about the same notorious discotheque (during which not a single DJ is either mentioned, shown, or interviewed; instead, the producers decided to titillate their audiences with sound bites by and about celebrities of the period in compromising situations involving sex, crime, and drugs). This type of lopsided reporting and historicizing is all the more noteworthy as it is accompanied by a remarkably consistent marginalization, even absence, of the music and the dance, those elements that form the core of disco and its various musical offspring and represent the blueprint for today's urban social dance culture. In the case of disco, even of social dance in general, popular memory seems curiously selective. Could this be because the sound of disco and post-disco music is essentially black, and its sensibility essentially gay? And because things black and things gay are still having trouble being marketed on Broadway, on TV, even in print? Let's remember that John Travolta's character in *Saturday Night Fever* is neither African American nor gay.

Indeed, if we also remember that in the United States, the discourse on both African Americans and gays as segments of American society has long been marked by periods of either sensationalism or social pathology (at times both), it isn't really surprising that the overall tone of the recent treatments of things disco (and, to some extent, post-disco) has tended to be correspondingly sensationalistic and/or pathological. It appears that many producers and writers, even in academic quarters, continue to pursue an almost obsessive interest in the deviant elements of night life—often at the expense of the music and the dance—but pay little attention to the creators and consumers of disco, house, or rave music, the dancers, and the DJs. In all, the majority of the current crop of treatments of disco and post-disco phenomena has done little to supply its harvesters with enough historical context to do the subject justice. By and large, those who were instrumental in creating the disco phenomenon, as well as those who carry their torch today are still being denied recognition.

With this book, I offer a corrective vision of urban dance culture in the late twentieth century. This vision is based on the premise that the marginality of disco and post-disco culture in the United States, and their combined impact on popular culture nationwide and beyond deserve more than the traditional cocktail of social pathology and sensationalism. By looking at popular music and social dance as parts of one cultural whole, I aim to give due recognition to the African American imprint on urban popular culture, both of the past and of the present. By focusing on New York, a city long central in shaping both popular music and social dance forms (often simultaneously, and on a national and international level), I contribute to the as yet unwritten history of social dance in twentieth-century America. While my focus oscillates between the larger historical context and a contemporary local scene, the central topic here is the post-disco underground, an environment that began to take shape in New York City more than a quarter of a century ago. At its core, it involves music, dancing, and marginal voices who insist on being heard.

Consequently, this account on underground dance music does not claim to be comprehensive, or to represent the last word on how disco emerged and developed, or how African American expressive culture supplied much of the musical and aesthetic material to an emerging gay community to help forge its own musical style and socio-cultural identity. Rather, I would like to situate this text at the nexus of two discussions, which, for reasons yet to be determined, have thus far tended to take place in separate arenas. Represented by two rapidly growing bodies of literature, both cultural studies and urban ethnography have only recently begun to treat the music-dance complex as a relevant topic. To the degree that this discourse has been altogether rather lively, it has also been somewhat disconnected and isolated. My aim here is to integrate. By drawing on ethnomusicology, American history, cultural studies, urban studies, and gay studies, as well as sociology and anthropology, I encourage those interested in music, dance, and interdisciplinary work to join me in recognizing and appreciating the remarkable contributions of several generations of participants in the urban social dance scene. When club DJs and dancers work, music and dance fuse as work becomes play. And it is through this play that we may understand the merits of the past while glimpsing the individual and collective potential yet to be realized. Keep on.

Acknowledgments

✯

While this book lists a single author, there are many people whose combined efforts helped make it a reality. I view this synthesis of all I have been taught about underground dance music in New York as a testimony to the spirit of giving and sharing of time, knowledge, skills, and most important, of music and the love of the music, on the part of all who got involved. My sincere thanks go to all who have thus been instrumental in shaping this account.

Heartfelt thanks go to all the people who helped me chart this territory, in innumerable conversations, interviews, references, suggestions, and by giving me access to people, places, and sources I would probably not have obtained otherwise: the dancers, DJs, party hosts and promoters, musicians, recording company and record pool personnel, 12-inch retailers, club management, and writers:

Steve Ward	Archie Burnett	Danny Tenaglia
Steven James	Frankie Knuckles	Louie Vega
Roy Davis	Darrin Friedman	James Bratton
John Hall	DJ Pierre	Alexis Suter
André Neal	Larry Flick	Yvonne Turner
Andy Panda	Todd Terry	Ricardo Hugh
Claire Dacey	Brian Chin	David Byron
Mark Finkelstein	Willie Ninja	Terence Hope
Victor Simonelli	Michael Taylor	Andy Reynolds
Ken Carpenter	Kenneth Williams Sr.	David Lozada
Kenny Gonzalez	Paul Biddle	Ceybil Jeffries
Marshall Swiney	Eve-Marie Breglia	Jephté Guillaume
Jayne Bond	Adam Goldstone	Phil D.
Dave Harrison	Stephanie Shepherd	Peter Schwartz
Michael Gomes	Cassio Ware	Aurelio Martin

Dan Pucchiarelli
Tim Richardson
John Robinson
Kevin Hedge
Freddie Perez
David Camacho
Bob Moss
Harry Soto
DJ Disciple
DJ Manski
Lisa Manning
Reynald Deschamps
Mel Cheren
Ken Johnston
Tyrone Francis
Gary Michael Wade
Jerel Black
Timothy Roberts
Arlene Yu
Costantino Padovano
Aaron Rosenberg
Dave DePino
Darren Ressler
Anthony Holland
Ralph Wilburn
Carlos Sanchez
Satoshi Tomie
George Morel
Will Straw
Benji Turner
Chris Payne

Tony Humphries
Mike DuPriest
Lionel Santana
Marco Navarra
Stan Hatzakis
Johnny Dynell
Craig Kallman
Kim Lightfoot
Christopher Gray
Frank Owen
Roger Sanchez
Sabrina Johnston
Barry Thomas
Little Ray
Barry "Bang" Thomas
Michael Paoletta
Mike Battin
Jhan Umali
Michael Gueli
Antonio Xtraordinaire
Bobby Judge
Michael Hope
Terence Hope
Ralphie Soler
John Poppo
Bari G.
Sarah Thornton
Tom Moulton
Rheji Burrell
Ronald Burrell
William Brennan

Victor Sanchez
Issa Jelani
Basil Thomas
Maurice Coleman
Barbara Tucker
Mia McLeod
Chat Boujo
Walter Gibbons
François Kevorkian
Moi Renée
Eric Green
Kris Flowers
Stephon Johnson
Allen Jeffrey
Troy Parrish
David Mancuso
Joe Claussell
Alex Smith
Steven Harvey
Joey Llanos
Al Mack
Nicky Siano
Kamati Pinkston
André Collins
Anthony Macaroni
Ricky Nelson
Jack Carroll
Francis Grasso
Manny Lehman
Brahms LaFortune
Syrus

I thank all those who offered critical input whenever I could not see the trees for the forest, during both the fieldwork and write-up phases: Anthony Barone, Karen Caesar-Brown, Renee Colwell, Steven Mamula, Niloofar Mina, David Patterson, Sviat Podstavsky, and Lois Wilcken. I am deeply indebted to my mentors: Lynn Chancer, Portia Maultsby, Francesca Rebollo-Sborgi, Adelaida Reyes Schramm, Sean Williams, Joe Blum, Dieter Christensen, Daniel Ferguson, Wolfgang Fikentscher, Peter Manuel, Robert O'Meally, and Mark Tucker. Thanks also to Chat Boujo, Gina Brown, John Carr, Travis Jackson, and David Patterson for their help with interview transcriptions and manuscript proofing, copying, and printing. I am also grateful for the advice and support of Elizabeth Davis and her staff at the Music Library of Columbia University throughout the duration of the project. I thank the editorial board at Wesleyan University for including this book in the Music/Culture Series, and especially Suzanna Tamminen and her staff for all their help in shaping the manuscript into a book.

A final bow of gratitude to all the dancers and DJs whose passion for music inspired this project, and gave me the energy to carry it through and the conviction that music and dance can be work, play, and art all at once—especially in the underground where the freedom to constantly redefine them is abundant. I therefore dedicate this book to the memory of those dancers and DJs who passed away during the ten years it took to complete this account. In this world, your feet no longer shuffle, your hands no longer spin the turntables. Your work, however, is still with us, shaping the way we still work—and we better work!

SIDE A

★

ONE

Introduction

★

"The definition of a track."
—The Black Rascals, New York Underground Records, 1988

"I came to New York City for its music." That has been my standard answer to the question as to my choice of residence. Initially, the music that drew me here was jazz. However, while pursuing a graduate degree in jazz studies in Manhattan, I visited a New York dance club, my first-ever visit to any sort of discotheque. The year was 1985, and the club was the Paradise Garage. But it wasn't until two years after the Garage closed its doors that I decided to embark on a study of club disc jockeys and their music, and not until 1990 that I formulated a systematic study of underground dance music (UDM) in New York City.

My interest in UDM had developed before I had any knowledge or understanding of the term. In the mid-1980s, my long-standing interest in rock and jazz music had somewhat declined, and I was searching for other types of music in which to get involved. I had been collecting 45 rpm singles and LPs in the areas of rock, jazz, pop, and their various subcategories since childhood, but was progressively less impressed by new releases. Upon relocating to New York City, however, I discovered house music—Chicago's electronic and minimalist offspring of disco music—in the form of a few 12-inch singles at a friend's apartment. The 12-inch single was a format that I had been aware of for only a few years. I had considered them a faddish novelty, not to be taken seriously by a record collector such as myself, and still viewed them with some suspicion. House, however, was a sound that grabbed my attention. After exploring the 12-inch phenomenon a little further, I found that it was only one of many categories subsumed under one overarching term: dance music. Yet, among these dance music 12-inch records, the ones that fascinated me most, particularly with regard to arrangement, sonority, and especially rhythmic complexity, were those categorized as house music, or club music.

The friend at whose apartment I had encountered the aforementioned singles then offered to take me to a dance club in lower Manhattan where he was a member—he called it a "disco." I was thus introduced to the Paradise Garage. and had my first taste of underground dance music without knowing what I was listening and dancing to. It wasn't quite the same music I'd heard on those 12-inch singles made in Chicago, but even more intriguingly, I was unable to identify a single record the disc jockey was playing during my first hour of being there. To a diehard music aficionado like me, this represented a formidable challenge. During the next two years before the Paradise Garage closed, I returned several times and began to familiarize myself with the music by building an extensive library of 12-inch dance music singles that now dwarfs my LP and 45 collection.

Discovering the underground: Entry to the field

I finished my jazz studies and enrolled in a graduate program in ethnomusicology. New York's jazz scene was still interesting, but my newfound passion led me increasingly away from jazz clubs and into dance clubs. For my doctoral dissertation, I decided to focus on house and club music, and the New York–based venues where this music was performed by disc jockeys,[1] such as the Paradise Garage. Entry to this field appeared difficult at first. I was interested in the workings of the dance music industry, but, as I found out, this industry was not particularly open to curious outsiders. After several requests for internships with recording studios and recording companies were turned down, a casual conversation became a turning point.

Terrence was not unlike myself: young, middle-class, heterosexual, and, as both a fan and performer of contemporary popular music, keenly interested in the workings of the music industry in New York City. We had met during a performance he and friends had put on for inner-city teenagers enrolled in a tutorial program sponsored by Columbia University. Since then we had compared notes on our musical tastes and approaches. We met on campus one afternoon for the purpose of his giving me some phone numbers he had in the local record industry, and for me to listen to and evaluate a demo of his latest r&b composition.

During this meeting, Terrence told me of his experience as a promoter in the local nightclub industry. While I busily jotted down potentially useful names and phone numbers, Terrence suddenly paused, looked straight at me and asked, "What kind of phone numbers do you really want? Just industry people, or underground people?"

At first, I was at a loss for an answer. I had already tried to communicate to him that I was not out to study the popular music industry of New York

City, an area, I sensed, vital to his own ambitions. As the term "under-ground" was new to me, I said something to the effect that I was not so much interested in major label contacts as in those connected to the world of dance clubs in the city, and mentioned my introduction to this scene some years ago by visiting the Paradise Garage. At this, Terrence nodded, "You want the underground."

Replaying this conversation in my mind, I discovered the significance of Terrence's comment. He was of course correct; more important, the "underground" he had put before me was the cultural domain I had been trying in vain to identify for some time. Here was the potential solution to the problem of defining the research domain of my thesis. Was underground a concept that applied to music as well as dance, to people as well as clubs, to a sound as well as an attitude? If so, underground could be re-garded and studied as a cultural entity within New York City, with invis-ible, yet distinct boundaries to be discovered. Soon after this conversation, the concept of a New York–specific underground dance music became cen-tral to my research.

The object of investigation: Underground dance music

The choice of underground dance music (UDM) in New York City de-serves some explanation. The prefix "underground" does not merely serve to explain that the associated type of music—and its cultural context—are familiar only to a small number of informed persons. Underground also points to the sociopolitical function of the music, framing it as one type of music that in order to have meaning and continuity is kept away, to a large degree, from mainstream society, mass media, and those empowered to en-force prevalent moral and aesthetic codes and values. As a systematic piece of inquiry, this study, for example, is more part of this mainstream than it is not. In contrast, the nature of the object of investigation is essentially an-tagonistic to academic inquiry. While this antagonism is a fundamental premise of much (cross-)cultural work, it is of particular relevance as a premise to this research project. The opposing natures of academic re-search on the one hand, and of UDM as research topic on the other thus form an a priori condition of this project.

A second consideration is equally critical. As dance music, UDM is so closely linked to dancing as a physical activity—which in turn is so directly connected and complementary to the affective force of music as sound— that the two central components, music and dance, should be understood as equally important halves of one single culturally specific concept. This concept is embedded in many African cultures.[2] By extension, it also applies to African American culture, which provides the context for UDM. In other words, as a musical arena in which dance and music hold equal weight, UDM is essentially African American in character.

Third, as a musical category of the 1980s and 1990s, UDM developed out of the disco phenomenon of the 1970s. Disco, to be discussed in more detail later, in turn emerged from a variety of musical influences, among them gospel, rhythm and blues, acid rock, and European electronic music. Another similarity to disco lies in UDM's core audience which is predominantly African American and Latino, male, and gay. And as was the case with disco, UDM's protagonists are DJs and record producers, while its institutions are the discotheque or club, the independent record company, the record pool, and the specialty retail store. Indeed, disco and UDM could be seen as essentially the same, if it weren't for two differences. First, disco is firmly associated with the decade *preceding* the emergence of UDM. Second, during that period, disco achieved temporary mainstream success on a scale so far denied to UDM.

Stylistically, house music, the predominant musical category of UDM, is closely related to disco music of the 1970s. A similar relationship can be applied to the respective dance styles, dance fashions, and dance environments. As will be discussed, the concept for the discotheque was imported from Europe as a musical environment characterized by a selective crowd dancing to recorded music provided by a DJ. On the other hand, as a weekly ritual through which marginality (whether black, Latino and/or gay) can be affirmed and celebrated within an urban setting through music and dance, disco is the creation of a New York–based group of primarily gay and/or minority men. Over a span of about thirty years, this segment of the population of New York City has redefined the art of combining sound and movement, style and statement, aesthetics and social politics. Indeed, many traits and trends—both musical and extramusical—now found throughout mainstream popular culture, were initially developed in the milieu of disco/UDM.

Although its roots are in 1960s' rhythm and blues, soul, and rock music, UDM is essentially a post-1970s, post-disco phenomenon, based in New York, and primarily shaped by the collective input of a sizable, yet limited number of predominantly gay African American and Latino men who view who they are and what they do in relation and response to dominant moral and aesthetic codes and values of late twentieth-century U.S. American society. In reaction (and often opposition) to this so-called mainstream, their music and dance is cultivated outside the view of the general public eye, in a cultural environment referred to as "underground." On the dance floor of an underground dance venue, away from the scrutinizing eye of society, a vision of an alternative and more egalitarian society can be pursued, tested, revised, experimented with. On any given weekday night in New York City (but mainly on weekends), this vision, hedonistic to some, utopian to others, is expressed in the ongoing quest for new ways to combine music with music, music with dancing, and at times, music with dancing, drugs, and sex.

Why study underground dance music? The role of New York City

I became interested in exploring the following four aspects of UDM: (1) the relationship between music and dance; (2) the relationship between music and "marginality;" (3) the cult and culture of the DJ, that is, the development and overlap of the roles of the DJ as musician, producer, performer, gatekeeper, authority figure, and artist; and (4) music as primary identifier of each of an array of urban subcultures,[3] with UDM as subject of a case study and New York City as example of a complex and heterogeneous urban context.

During the 1980s, as part of the mainly economic and demographic changes affecting the industries and markets of popular music in the United States,[4] a variety of local underground scenes[5] developed in urban environments around the country. Often, these local scenes were and are characterized by typical dance music styles. Over time, some of these scenes have broadened their influence toward national proportions, such as hip-hop (from the Bronx) and grunge rock (from Seattle); others remained limited to local appeal, such as go-go in Washington, D.C., and bass in Miami.[6]

Among these urban enclaves, New York City holds a special place, even beyond its dual role as center of the national music industry and as creative hotbed. Here, instead of one dominant musical culture, many coexist, with artists ranging from only local appeal (for example, showcase rock bands)[7] to those with national and international exposure (for example, hip-hop artists who feed on the underground tradition established by their older, Bronx-bred colleagues).[8]

As evident from these few examples, music has become a primary marker of local urban subcultures. While this may be true on a worldwide scale,[9] the examples that can be encountered within U.S. borders are many. New York City is but one instance of an urban enclave having come to be associated not only with specific ethnic groups, but with musical categories (often referred to as styles) as well. Studies of this particular type of relationship between music and the city are still rare, especially those that attempt a comparative approach.

This study attempts to sort out the ties of UDM to New York City as a unique urban environment. It examines the role of UDM as a primary marker of a particular local musical culture that shares the locale of New York City with other local musical cultures; at the same time its influence is felt around the globe, particularly within other urban centers where other worlds of underground dancing exist.[10]

Music and marginality

Marginality is understood here as a social status marked by a condition of ongoing negotiation with, and/or reaction or opposition to, one culturally defined dominant system of values and beliefs, by one or several so-called subcultures that rank lower in terms of cultural power. This negotiation or opposition may come in a variety of forms of (sub-)cultural expression, and through it, hidden or unresolved contradictions of the dominant "mainstream" culture may be highlighted and transformed.[11] Marginality is thus linked to such concepts as culture, subculture, counter culture, hegemony, style, and identity.[12] Music is one of the more powerful vehicles for expressing marginality culturally, to the extent that musical characteristics have come to define certain cultures.[13] In New York City, UDM is one way to express and celebrate cultural and social marginality.

The relationship between music, especially as musical practice or behavior, on the one hand, and social and cultural marginality as an extramusical context on the other, is still insufficiently studied. It can be grouped under the umbrella of "music and identity." Discussions of this nexus have been lively in recent years and have resulted in a still growing body of literature. However, within this discussion, studies of music and its relationship to marginality remain rare.[14] With regard to the marginalization of African American and gay cultures in modern American society (both "core cultures"[15] of UDM) studies of the role of music in these processes are next to nonexistent.

The purpose of a study of underground dance music

In terms of subject matter, this study focuses on a largely unexplored terrain of musicking.[16] In the context of UDM, the DJ acts as central figure in an environment defined by a dynamic interaction between himself as the person in charge of the DJ booth and the dancers who, as collective body, are in charge of the dance floor. The DJ, as soundscape architect, constructs a musical program from preproduced, prerecorded sources, mostly 12-inch vinyl records, and, via a powerful sound system that he controls as well, feeds it to an ever-shifting group of dancers who, on the dance floor, in proximity of the DJ booth, translate "his"[17] music into "their" dance, his "working" into their "working (out)." The feedback between booth and floor is bi-directional and results in a continuous negotiation of power and energy (referred to as "vibe") which can take hours to reach a climactic peak. A successful DJ can peak his floor many times during a night of dancing, depending on his grasp and interaction with the most responsive and enthusiastic dancers who may in turn draw in others.

Despite a growing body of literature on contemporary dance music and its practitioners, this type of musicking is still not very well understood. The associated cultural terrain is marked by a terminology of terms—disco, discotheque, club, house, 12-inch single, mixing, remixing, spinning, working—whose meanings are still vague and ill-defined after years of use (and abuse) in the popular press: In contrast to other rather well studied strains of African American musical culture, such as jazz and blues, UDM, together with disco and house as related musical categories, topically still represents a white spot on the map of American music in this century, and a lacuna in musicological analysis.

A definition of underground

The prefix "underground" often denotes a context in which certain activities take place out of a perceived necessity for a protected, possibly secret arena that facilitates opposition, subversion, or delimitation to a larger, dominant, normative, possibly oppressive environment. These environments may be political, social or cultural in nature, and underground responses to them may emphasize one of these qualities or combine them in various ways. A few examples of underground scenes and movements help illustrate this point.

Up to the present day, in countries where freedom of the press is either not granted or perceived to be restricted, various avenues for the production and distribution of an underground press continue to be created.[18] In the United States, the Underground Railroad, initiated by Harriet Tubman, became a concerted effort by people of African descent to gain freedom from slavery and oppression in America.[19] More recently, in association with the counterculture of the 1960s, the concept of underground was deemed central enough to be included in the title of an anthology analyzing the social and political implications of the latter.[20]

As a concept with political and cultural implications, underground has been attached to musical practices outside the United States as well. In the U.S.S.R. prior to the Gorbachev government, rock music and the associated youth culture were largely underground.[21] In the United States, at various points in time, and for various reasons, various forms of music have been cultivated in an underground environment. While not exclusive to forms of African American music (as the example of the underground culture centered around death metal illustrates), the music of worship among slaves during the formation of early Black churches,[22] and of jazz[23] were at times marked by underground characteristics. In a musical underground, dissemination may occur through unorthodox conduits or media, as in the case of a network of Pullman porters who, prior to World War II, acted as distributors of early "race music" records, or of rhythm and blues radio thereafter[24] (or of the death metal underground, which became accessible in the 1990s via public access television).

Elsewhere in urban and suburban America, sizable followings of underground hip-hop and underground dance music have formed since the 1980s.[25] Specific to New York City, the label underground has long referred to a socio-cultural avant-garde that, since the 1950s has included beat poets, performance artists, painters, and musicians ranging from Lou Reed's group The Velvet Underground to downtown drag chanteuse Chi Chi Valenti.[26] In American society, in response to the combined trauma resulting from the assassinations of Attorney General Robert Kennedy, civil rights leader Martin Luther King Jr., and the bloodshed at the Altamont Festival and Kent State University, underground, in the early 1970s, became a label common to environments where the ideas of social change could be further cultivated. Many examples of this change came in the form of artistic expressions, including music, which has long been a vehicle for ideas of social progress, particularly among African Americans.[27]

In sum, underground activities, whether primarily political or cultural in nature (some are both) can be said to take place in a limited space, inhabited by a limited number of participants who may establish various mechanisms to further the longevity of their activities. One of the most common of such mechanisms is the cultivation and control of insider knowledge. Musical conoisseurship is one of the attributes of underground membership.

A definition of dance music

Dance music is not simply music for dancing, as in the general sense of the word, which without any specific association of context or characteristics could refer to a Viennese waltz, a Renaissance saltarello, or a Cuban mambo. Throughout this account, however, dance music has a specific meaning. It is a locally and historically defined musical term of the 1980s that was coined and has been used since by the American music industry (especially its trade press) to replace the category of disco.

Disco, the dominant sound of mass music in the second half of the 1970s,[28] became a victim of its success in the face of racism and homophobia.[29] As a description of musical style, the term disco fell quickly into disuse; if used now, it has primarily historical and often negative associations. Beginning in the late 1970s and early 1980s, these associations have often been expressed both in disparaging remarks aimed at the music (such as "This music sucks," "It's cheap and has no inherent value") as well as the associated milieu ("Disco is faggot music" or "Disco people are superficial and do a lot of drugs").[30] In the United States, the disco backlash, as emotional as the disco craze that had spawned it, culminated in 1979 in a public record burning, orchestrated by rock radio DJ Steve Dahl in a Chicago basketball stadium to the chant of thousands: "Disco sucks!"[31]

Whether or not this incident symbolized the death of disco as a mainstream enterprise, after 1980 the term disco did in fact gradually vanish from the public arena. As a cultural expression, however, disco lived on, cherished by those who had invested perhaps the most meaning into it and derived the most pleasure from it. While it would be incorrect here to dismiss the roles of gay communities in other cities, they do not compare in national importance to that of New York City. Here, disco was transformed in the same underground milieu from which it had initially sprung: that of marginalized urban, young, gay, black and Latino men.

In the early 1980s, to counteract the association of disco with homosexuality and ethnic minorities, the label "dance music" was quickly embraced by the recording industry and its consumers as a more neutral term. It was also more vague. Consequently, dance music became less of a stylistic marker than disco had been. Many artists associated with varied styles of pop and rock had released disco records in the 1970s. Indeed, this "jumping on the bandwagon" is often seen as part of disco's demise in the first place. However, under the banner of dance music, a continuation of this practice was less controversial. A record from practically any pop style, ranging from rhythm and blues to rock to new wave[32], could and can become classifiable under dance music. The main prerequisite is not a matter of style or authenticity, but form: since the late 1970s, the 12-inch single has become the main format in the disco/dance market. That a song is issued (or, as was and is often the case, reissued) on a 12-inch makes it dance music.

The use of the general term "dance music" for a specific category of popular music was therefore probably a conscious decision made within the record industry. Still, as much as the neutralizing effect was desired, the connection to disco remains, especially in New York. Here, dance music carries as much a post-disco connotation as a anti-disco connotation. Many who have lived through the disco era, especially veteran DJs and dancers, consider all UDM essentially disco music.

By definition, then, dance music, in its specific meaning, is associated with the medium of the 12-inch single. This association links a stylistically vague category to an industry at the center of which stands the DJ. The DJ became a new type of cultural hero and arbiter in the 1970s, and continued in this fashion through the 1980s and 1990s. New York DJs were at the forefront of establishing not only the 12-inch single as a new recording format and commodity, but were instrumental in establishing those institutions that are now associated with the dance music industry: the record pool, the specialty retail store (where 12-inch singles are sold, sometimes exclusively), the independent record company[33] with an emphasis on dance music repertoire, and the discotheque or club as a location where the level of technological sophistication of audio sound amplification is continually expanded.

Dance music should be understood as an umbrella term. It embraces several categories of music—among them, garage, hi-NRG (pronounced "high energy"), disco, eurodisco, house and its many subcategories (acid house, deep house, hard house, tribal house), techno, trance, classics—that have in common the 12-inch single as primary product format. Lumped together as dance music, all these categories are associated with the DJ in the important role of cultural broker regarding their production and consumption. Therefore, dance music may be considered "canned" or "mediated" music.[34] The medium of the 12-inch single, created primarily by DJs for DJs and other dance enthusiasts, is the primary sound carrier format of dance music.

The relationship of underground dance music to New York City

There exist in New York City many places to go dancing, and many 12-inch dance singles are produced, marketed, and sold here that are not underground in character, nor are they played in underground dance clubs exclusively. However, in contrast to these institutions, variously labeled as "commercial," "mainstream," or "tourist," the underground dance club, and by extension the culture associated with it, has been treated as a type of cultural security zone for decades by three groups that have long been on the margins of American society: African Americans, Latinos, and persons who describe themselves as either lesbian or gay. The dance underground in New York City has been and continues to be defined essentially by the input from members of these urban populations.

As much as underground dance music is referred to as music for or by gays,[35] or blacks and Latinos, or both, its culture is simultaneously related to African-derived expressive culture[36] and gay culture. As stated earlier, the majority of the music played by DJs at underground dance clubs is identified as house, which has its roots in the black gay scene of urban Chicago during the late 1970s and early 1980s.[37] The majority of those who identify themselves as participants of the New York dance underground are either minority (primarily black or Latino) or gay, or both. This includes most of the well-known DJs. The record industry that caters to this relatively small urban market is largely made up of people who view themselves as marginal to a record industry (again labeled "mainstream" or "commercial") that focuses its attention chiefly on the pop market. As recently as the late 1980s, the displacement of vinyl by CDs as standard sound carrier format in the pop market has highlighted and confirmed the overall marginal position of the dance music industry. In the New York underground, vinyl remains the favored product, as its DJs (who frequently refer to themselves as "vinyl junkies") are the primary record buying group. Vinyl records, once a mainstream commercial product, in the 1990s have been ascribed marginal status. In the recording industry, the word "underground" is increasingly used to describe a marginal or nonmainstream product, performer, or audience. In the context of dance music in New York, underground refers not only to a cultural, but also to an economic margin.

In the context of social dancing in New York City, underground is thus a complex term, with historical, social, cultural, and political implications. As a prefix to UDM, it relates to the ascribed and perceived marginality of its patrons. The attribute "underground" highlights the role of race, gender, and sexual orientation as expressed through stylistic means (including music and dance, but also fashion and language) that are cultivated largely outside of the awareness of the American mainstream, let alone its media. To dance in the underground is to view dancing as both individual and collective performance, with the latter including the DJ as both performer and individual artist. "Clubbing" in New York's underground—which involves not only participation on the dance floor, but also all preparations and post-dance activities—is a musical ritual enacted primarily in music and dance.[38]

Both components of underground dance music are connected to New York City as locale. Underground dance culture developed here, with local African American and Latino gay men at the helm. As New York City became a national center for the emerging Gay Liberation movement, it also became the disco capital of the world. At this time, New York discotheques became important social institutions not just to the general urban population, but to the gay segment in particular. In 1975, the 12-inch single was conceived by a New York DJ. Some twenty years later, New York DJs travel to European and Asian cities as invited guests, bringing with them a selection of 12-inch records (some of which were produced in New York) to play in clubs that may emulate, by name or architectural and acoustic design, famous New York dance venues.[39] New York remains not only a center of the national recording industry, but the center of the national dance market: most American independent dance music recording companies are located in New York.[40] Geographically and historically, New York City is an integral element of UDM. The aesthetics, the history, the protagonists, and institutions of UDM and its cultural context are all connected to this locale.[41]

What qualities make this music a part of New York's underground dance scene? Variously labeled "underground," "dance music," "underground dance music" or "club music" by its patrons, it is, as they put it, different from the music summarily referred to as rock or pop.[42] Some call it "house music" or simply "house," but are quick to acknowledge the existence of similar and/or related categories, such as "club," "garage," "jersey," "classics," "trance," "acid house," "deep house," "progressive house," "tribal," "jungle," "hard house," or "hi-NRG." Many of these labels, while used to describe stylistic differences, can be subsumed under the category of underground to distinguish it from commercial or mainstream product—which in turn is associated with labels such as "pop music" or "radio music."

Whereas the latter is accessible at the national and international level, through mainstream media, such as radio, TV, and record store chains, underground dance music is not only heard almost exclusively at local dance clubs, it is available to the public only locally, in the form of 12-inch singles, at specialty retail stores catering to amateur and professional DJs. Its authors/producers are frequently the same DJs who play these records at a dance venue that may be only several blocks away from the record store, or from the location of the recording studio where they have recorded and mixed the music for the record, perhaps earlier in the same day or week.

The audience for this music reflects the heterogeneity of the population of New York City. UDM's audience is more ethnically mixed than those of various categories of rock and pop. It is also decidedly non-teenage, and predominantly African American and gay, with a smattering of Latinos, Caucasians, and Asians. Interestingly, this music, and its sociocultural context, are largely ignored by the national mass media, the popular press, newspapers, music magazines, radio and television, national academic programs, institutions, and publications. It has been and may very well continue to be connected to New York City for quite a while. UDM is therefore locally specific. Among these local specificities, those of a social and cultural nature are of special relevance.

The questions this study addresses are: How is UDM and its cultural environment shaped by the relationship between gay culture and black culture in New York City? What is that relationship and what role does UDM play in it? What role does UDM play in the context of a positive affirmation of social and cultural marginality, be it gay, black, or both? How do issues of race, ethnic identity, gender, and sexuality factor in?

Mediated music and musical immediacy

While musical immediacy remains the basic model for musicking around the globe, technological innovation with regard to sound, particularly in the Western world, has made possible a division across space and time between the processes of producing and consuming music.[43] Through the development of such technologies as the radio, the phonograph, the television, and the computer, "musical immediacy" is no longer a sine qua non, but rather an option.[44] The audio technology that allows for arbitrary storage, manipulation, and reproduction of musical sound has shaped a contemporary soundscape characterized by mediated music; that is, musical sound being reproduced independent of the conditions of its initial production.

Historically, as it became possible to capture sound on wire, shellac, vinyl, tape, and disc, the processes of musical production and consumption changed in essence. No longer were they married to each other by the immediacy of time and space. As independent processes they could be further subdivided: production into pre-production, production, and reproduction; consumption into public or private, foregrounded, or active (say, in a concert setting) versus backgrounded, or passive (Muzak, for example).

The widespread use of mediated music, particularly in Western societies, has of course not displaced the concept of musical immediacy. On the streets of New York City, street musicians compete not only with each other, but with the portable radios, cassette and CD players many members of their potential audience carry. In the area of popular music in particular, many forms of overlap between immediate (usually referred to as "live") and mediated types of music have emerged over time. The playback technique, nowadays a common practice, is but one example where selected features of both types are combined. As phenomena associated with popular music gradually caught the interest of some musicologists, the coexistence of musical immediacy and mediated music became an issue that called for differentiated modes of analysis.[45] These apply in the case of UDM as an example of performance where musical immediacy and mediated music coexist by definition.

The music-dance relationship in social dance

While understood and often acknowledged as related areas of human expression, music and dance are often treated as phenomena distinct from each other. Until recently, scholars in the fields of music and dance tended to view their respective terrains as, while not mutually exclusive, still sufficiently dissimilar to warrant an academic structure reflective of a predominantly separatist philosophy. Accordingly, the study of music has traditionally been assigned to musicologists or ethnomusicologists, whereas dance has been the domain of dance anthropology, dance ethnology, or ethnochoreology.[46] Often, this academic division is extended to the level of gender.[47] Men generally outnumber women in music departments; the reverse is true of many academic dance departments. Noteworthy in this context is the concomitant difference in status and scholarly position between music and dance scholars within the general American academy. While musicology can look back on a long-standing (if underfunded) tradition of scholarship, dance studies, while suffering similar budgetary constraints, have received little respect as academic subject.[48]

The idea that dance is often integral to any given musical culture has only recently begun to be viewed as essential to understanding the culture as a whole.[49] At the same time, the performance of music, as opposed to music as artifact, authoritative text, or sounded object, has long been a central focus of inquiry. In the context of UDM, a musical performance not only manifests the music as sounded reality ("making music come to life," to paraphrase DJ David DePino), it also connects the musical sound to the dimension of musical experience or sensation on the part of those involved in the performance, including those participants described as performers, musicians, dancers, or audiences. This connection, while not always associated with the concept of performance, links up with the use of musical instruments (including the human voice) by musicians (professional or not), and with the use of the human body, as an instrument of musical expression responding to musical sound produced outside the body through movement (except in those instances when the singer is also a dancer). However, while the examples where music and dance are elements of one and the same performance context are legion, the literature that examines how music and dance relate to each other in context is comparatively scant.[50] Using UDM as an example, I shall return to this complex of issues in chapters 3 and 4.

Research phases

This study of UDM is based in large part on ethnographic fieldwork, most of which was undertaken during 1991–93, with additional follow-up research undertaken in 1994, 1995, and 1999. Initial forays and preliminary test and survey studies took place from 1988 to 1990. Notwithstanding internet connections to local dance scenes in Chicago, San Francisco, and London, all participant-observation research took place in New York City, primarily in Manhattan.

From a hindsight perspective, this research project can be divided into four phases. The first lasted from 1985 until 1989, and includes my first encounter with house music in recorded form, my introduction to New York dance clubs, and initial forays into New York as the setting for several pilot studies in urban ethnomusicology, all of which were connected to graduate coursework in anthropology and ethnomusicology. The second phase consisted of the formulation of a dissertation research proposal in ethnomusicology, with a focus on dance music and the dance music industry in New York City. This proposal was accepted by a departmental committee in April 1991. The third phase was an extended period of fieldwork, beginning with an internship with *Dance Music Report* in late 1991, a New York–based trade paper serving the national dance music industry. This phase, while marked by interruptions in 1995 and 1997, was the longest, overlapping with the fourth and last phase. Between the fall of 1998 and the summer of 1999, a series of follow-up interviews and club visits took place. As of November 1992, a fourth phase of write-up began while the emphasis on fieldwork temporarily diminished. Phases 3 and 4, however, have overlapped since then. Because New York City was the location for both fieldwork and write-up, there was no break in the contacts between researcher and researched, some of whom have become friends.

Ethnography and ethnohistory: A brief detour

Any sound ethnographic methodology should come to terms with the time dimension of its topic.[51] This raises the issue of the relationship between a diachronic and a synchronic treatment. These approaches, while mutually exclusive in scope, may be used simultaneously in writing. Because they draw on and complement each other, they have the potential to improve data categorization and analysis.

The methods of ethnography that are generally based on data gathered in a relatively short time span (a few years at most) can do only so much to explain the state of affairs of a certain musical style or scene at a particular point in time. As both the topic under investigation and its context are dynamic entities, little in the way of scientific truths can be pronounced beyond the window of time allotted for the study. This is why I believe that ethnography can benefit from ethnohistory, which usually concerns itself with larger time spans (decades or even centuries). Both approaches have advantages and pitfalls, but a combination of both, attempted in this study, seems to promise the highest beneficial yield.

Ethnohistory is of particular relevance in situations where traditional sources for the documentation of historic developments are scarce and/or difficult to come by. This applies to the study of UDM for several reasons. First, the cultural context of UDM is still essentially nondocumented, based on its underground status. The tradition that contains the knowledge and value system of UDM is essentially oral, and therefore unsuitable for written fixation. Second, UDM is part of a long-standing African American musical tradition that, to a large degree, is also based on orality. Third, as much as mainstream America was swept by disco fever in the late 1970s, the bad taste of the Disco Sucks! movement had a lasting effect, to the extent that seemingly anything to do with disco, even the term itself, was gradually removed from the public eye (especially in the United States) by the early 1980s. A review of the literature, to be discussed in the following chapter, bears this out. Not until the mid-1990s did disco reenter the public sphere in the form of television specials, Hollywood films, and a style nostalgia focusing on disco wear and the myth of Studio 54. A discussion of disco and its emergence from and return to a sociocultural underground is therefore necessary to an understanding of UDM in New York City.

TWO

Disco

The Premise for Underground Dance Music

"Ain't No Stoppin' Us Now."
—McFadden and Whitehead, Philadelphia International Records, 1979

Literature on disco and dance music

When I began researching post-disco dance music in New York, books on disco and disco-related dance music appeared close to nonexistent. The few that did were out of print. A decade later, with the resurgence of disco-era paraphernalia, the release of a few movies built around disco themes and of a slew of CD disco compilations, both the disco era and the DJ phenomenon it gave birth to have received notably more attention. While trade books and documentary films recently have been increasing in number, one still has to turn to disciplines such as sociology, history, cultural studies, or American studies for treatments with a comprehensive, analytical, or non-journalistic bent. The picture is equally bleak in ethnomusicology and in the field of dance studies, with gay studies faring slightly better.

Until the publication of Poschardt's *DJ Culture* in 1995 (unavailable in English until 1998), Haden-Guest's *The Last Party: Studio 54, Disco, and the Culture of the Night* in 1997, and Jones and Kantonen's *Saturday Night Forever: The Story of Disco* in 1999, the last commercially available books devoted to disco music and/or New York City as America's dance music capital appeared on the U.S. market in 1978 and 1980 (both now out of print). Goldman's *Disco* (1978) provides a spotty and anecdotal account of the New York disco scene, preceded by a valuable, but poorly documented history of social dancing in twentieth-century America. Miezitis' *Night Dancin'* (1980) is the result of a thirty-day tour-de-force through New York City's nightlife, with some ethnographic trimmings in the form of pictures, interviews and an organization of the material into three categories (music, people, style) that gives evidence of an attempt of social analysis. Perhaps the most comprehensive account of disco's grip on the national music industry is Radcliffe Joe's *This Business of Disco* (1980). The author, disco editor at *Billboard* magazine at the time, presents an exhaustive sweep over most facets of the disco industry, including its emergence, main institutions, impact on other media and forms of music, including its links to organized crime. Since then, the attempts to fill a glaring void have highlighted the dearth of disco-related literature all the more: In 1985, Doug Shannon, a former DJ from Cleveland, Ohio, published an ambitious manual on disco as an economic enterprise. Although comprehensive in scope, it joins Joe's book by unilaterally focusing on disco as a product-driven market. The disco consumer, and the ways in which disco is consumed are either mentioned in passing only, or else are tacitly taken for granted.

Until recently, there has been next to no literature on the connections among discotheques, gay culture, and New York City (the latter both as a gay mecca and the capital of disco). This noteworthy paucity has elevated the role of a now rapidly growing number of pertinent articles in either print (or, more precisely, out-of-print) and, increasingly, on the Internet. Because these sources serve as platforms of cultural information in specifically gay or otherwise underground or alternative cultures, they have been treated as primary sources for this book.

Magazines and newspapers such as *Out/Look, Gay Times, Vibe,* the *New York Times, New York,* or the *Village Voice* are or were at one point urban institutions particular either to New York, or to gay or underground culture in general, with some possible overlap. In some cases, the authors writing for these outlets became consultants for this study. A special mention must be made of Harvey's "Behind The Groove. New York City's Disco Underground," an article that appeared in the September 1983 issue of the British underground magazine *Collusion* and was reprinted in the 11 March 1994 issue of the British magazine *DJ.* In addition to a short historical overview, the author offers transcriptions of interviews with six of "New York's top mixers and DJs," the first instance of an undertaking of this kind. The combination of disco and underground in the article's subtitle as the first printed instance of the term "underground" used in connection with dance music in New York is particularly noteworthy.

Apart from literary sources of this kind, the pickings are slim. Besides the odd commercial book release, a handful of academic treatments of the same cultural arena are of special value. They are summarily described as follows. Based on the available literature, the history of dance music—more specifically the history of music and dance in the context of social dancing—is spotty. Relevant to this study, however, is the agreement by many scholars on the importance of the African cultural influence on social dance forms in America, especially when understood in a historical continuum.[1] The premises on which most of these authors base their efforts have been succinctly formulated by Clark in her dissertation "Rock Dance in the United States, 1960–1970," which, in the words of the author, is inherently conceived as an "explication of cultural patterns within which [U.S. American] social dance forms [that] developed between 1910 and 1970."[2]

The analysis provided by scholars writing on social dance alleviates to some degree some of the spotty histories provided by authors writing on disco specifically. Before I turn to these works, I want to emphasize the cultural thread that links earlier forms and worlds of social dance in the United States to the disco and post-disco eras. Clark's statement concerning the pervasive appeal of the Twist in 1961 applies equally to disco dancing and clubbing from the 1970s to the present day, an indication of an ongoing Africanization of American culture that has not yet been fully acknowledged or understood: "When the Twist did break full-scale across the nation,[3] the general public was dancing an African-derived dance motif, to African-derived music, taught to them by an African-derived American. From 1619 to 1961 was a lengthy period of acculturation indeed!"[4] The data for the present study suggest that this period is ongoing.

The impression is that, almost without exception, there has been no substantial and/or easily accessible study of urban musical cultures defined by or associated with social dancing in the United States undertaken and/or published in the last twenty years. This scarcity in turn highlights the role of these exceptions[5] and those of unpublished and/or less substantial studies.

Anthony Thomas's concise "The Gay Black Imprint on American Dance Music," published in 1989 in the now defunct gay magazine *Out/Look*, is the reworking of his term paper "The House The Kids Built. The Music of a Black-American Subculture," written a year earlier at the Yale Divinity School for a course on Afro-American thought taught by Cornel West. In a footnote, Thomas is described as an amateur pop sociologist and dabbling DJ. He died in the early 1990s before I encountered his article, which has since been reprinted.[6]

Arlene Yu's B.A. thesis "'I Was Born This Way': Celebrating Community in a Black Gay Disco" was written at Radcliffe College, in 1988. It is one of the earliest ethnographic accounts of underground dance culture based on fieldwork, and valuable for its focus on one of the premier UDM institutions in New York City at the time, the Paradise Garage, where Yu, a professional dancer, did most of her fieldwork during a period of regular attendance in the mid-1980s.

Glenn A. Berry's M.A. thesis "House Music's Development and the

East-Coast Underground Scene," submitted in 1992 at the University of Wisconsin for a master's degree in Afro-American Studies, is another indication that the thematic complex around contemporary social dancing and music has so far attracted more interest from researchers trained in fields other than musicology or ethnomusicology. Based on a series of interviews with underground DJs (most of whom were based in metropolitan New York at the time), Berry's account indicates the range and variety of styles of, and approaches to, urban dance music in a decade after the decline of disco. Berry's work underscores the necessity to consider several categories of related literature, to which his study, strictly speaking, belongs.

Few as they are, these examples appear indicative of a trend. The topic of urban dance music in general, but within the above specific definition, has recently begun to attract interest from scholars of various fields, with varied backgrounds and interests.[7] These books and essays are valuable as additional references, as they help to situate the specificities of UDM in New York City within the context of disco and dance music culture elsewhere in the country and world. They also raise questions about the musicianship of club DJs, a topic often overlooked by writers focusing exclusively on radio DJs,[8] but nonetheless at the core of UDM. Before I begin my discussion of UDM proper, however, an outline of the historical connections of UDM and disco music is in order.

A definition of disco

The many definitions of the term "disco" are associated with a period during the 1970s when it became a label first referring to a specific musical environment, then to a type of popular music, and later to various styles of dress and hair and a leisure-time philosophy of extravagance, hedonism, and, to some, decadence.[9]

For the purposes of this chapter, however, disco will not refer to the amalgam of sociocultural phenomena comprising music, dance and style that are often associated with the disco boom or disco fever of the mid-to-late 1970s. The social and cultural development of disco before, during, and after that period will be discussed in chapter 6. Here, I am concerned with disco as a concept denoting a particular performance environment in which technologically mediated music is made immediate at the hands of a DJ, and in which this music is responded to via dance by bodies on the dance floor. I call this concept the disco concept. To understand the disco concept is to understand the conceptual and historical foundations of UDM. Disco is UDM's sine qua non.[10]

The word disco is the abbreviation for the French *discothèque*,[11] referring to an institution that, for the purpose of social dancing, was established long before the 1970s, with musical mediation—in the form of recordings of music for dancing—as its outstanding musical trait. Accordingly, a discotheque or disco may be defined as a circumscribed location, usually an indoor setting such as a basement, a loft, a converted mansion, restaurant, bar, garage, or warehouse, where an alternative or contrasting world to the one outside is created through the redesign of aural and visual perception, two of the main human senses in daily life. Inside a disco, the visual sense is often lessened through the use of (relative) darkness, while auditory perception is drastically heightened, through the constant presence of music at a high volume and a wide frequency spectrum. At times, this may result in the crossing of the boundary between music as sonic versus physical sensation. Indeed, this sensory blurring is often intentional. The music is performed not by traditional musicians, but rather by a DJ who determines its intensity, continuity, tempo, and style through choices of repertoire and program.

The DJ's audience is also active in creating the alternative world of a disco. Completing the definition of the disco concept is the disco environment, which prioritizes the aural dimension at the expense of the visual. Accordingly, a disco is visited, usually at nighttime, by a clientele that comes to socialize, drink (if a bar is included on the premises), smoke, and/or do drugs. Most important and visible, however, disco clients come to interact with a DJ's performance through dance. The nature of this dance is primarily social. To dance at a discotheque or club is tantamount to partaking in social dance. Above all, a disco is a place for social interaction in which music and dance are the essential elements.

Before turning to the history of disco as a phenomenon that, over a period of about a decade, oscillated between a local, New York–based underground and a nationwide commercial craze, I shall offer a brief look at other North American dance crazes that preceded disco. I hope that the resulting continuities and discontinuities may outline a rough history of American social dance in this century. If they do, it will help give disco its proper position in American popular culture. While this history has yet to be fully documented, it is not too early to speak of a continuum of social dance in the United States—ranging from the Charleston to the latest forms of underground club dancing, including b-boying, voguing, lofting, jacking, whacking, and freestyling—that has just begun to be acknowledged and studied. Disco is a part of this continuum, and its basic cultural imprint is African American.

urban — *dominant*
cultural origins of social dance
pattern

Social dance in America: The African American continuum

"The term social dance has been variously used to mean all dances designed to bring people together for group participation and enjoyment and in the twentieth century to refer to a specific type, namely ballroom. Under the broader use of the term, all dance when carried on for purposes of group participation and sociability may be referred to as social dance."[12] This definition, taken from a study of 1960s social dance forms in the United States, was written at a time when this particular form of social dance represented the latest permutation of popular or vernacular dance forms in twentieth century America. A second definition offered by the author makes the connection between American social dance and African American culture during most of the twentieth century explicit. As a premise to the present study, it is worth quoting here as well: "During the twenties, it was in the urban United States that the cultural values of American Negroes, at least manifested in their music and their dance, began to permeate and affect the values of the dominant American cultural pattern."[13]

This assessment is consistently confirmed by other historians of social dance in the United States.[14] According to Clark, the generic origin of almost every 1960s' rock dance motif is based on earlier social dances of Afro-American character. Writing in the early 1970s, she uses the category "rock dance" as the most fitting overall term for U.S.-based social dance during the decade preceding the disco era. Still, the following definition of rock dance is applicable to the dance forms of the subsequent disco and post-disco eras:

Rock dance is that dance which begins in time with the Twist and includes those social dances danced to rock music. More specifically, it includes those dances where partners do not touch and where locomotor patterns and designs are, for the most part, of secondary concern. The primary characteristic of rock dance is the use of various parts of the body in segmented, sequential, rhythmic action. . . . Beginning in 1960, these stylistic origins, regardless of form, have dominated social dance in the United States.[15]

If the polycentric use of the dancing body is not only a characteristic of underground dancing in the 1980s and 1990s (as it was of rock dancing in the 1960s), but also a characteristic of dance in sub-Saharan West Africa in general,[16] then this influence on American social dance may well be part of a cultural continuum of African origin reaching back beyond the turn of the century. By contrast, around 1910, the European imprint on American social dance appears to have diminished for good.[17]

It follows that "rock dance" and "underground dance" are more historically than culturally or stylistically differentiated terms. In its use of the body as expressive instrument, underground dancing can be understood as part of an American continuum of social dance styles that has been marked by a pervasive African American imprint at least since the 1920s.[18] There is a structural affinity between rock, disco, and post-disco dance styles, spanning a thirty-five year period since the arrival of the Twist as a symptom of "a changing scene in social dance."[19]

Changing scenes had also marked the period between the Charleston and the Twist as only two of many widely popular dances. Indeed, during the first half of the twentieth century, American society experienced several dance crazes.[20] In the 1930s, jazz was transformed from an originally exclusively African American genre into mainstream entertainment under the name "swing" (which referred to the music as much as to the dance), with New York City setting the trend for the rest of the nation. Based on the principal mode of musical delivery, many dance historians now consider World War II to represent the demarcation line between two periods of social dancing. Despite the availability of jukeboxes in bars, jook joints, and honky-tonks, the standard by which the quality of dance music was measured prior to World War II was based on the performance of dance bands or orchestras playing "live" on a podium, stage, or bandstand while the dancers took to the adjacent floor.

After World War II, particularly in the 1950s and 1960s, two factors combined to diminish the role of this form of dance music performance. One was the increase of costs needed to sustain dance orchestras; the other was the rapidly growing recording industry, accompanied by significant advances in recording and playback technologies. Stereophonic sound became a standard soon after its development in the 1950s, and following the radio and gramophone, television technology became quickly available to the mass consumer.[21] The combination of cost efficiency and high degree of technological sophistication can also be linked to the emergence of discotheques in the 1960s. By that time, an industry had been developed that supplied a steady flow of musical product to an audience whose ears had come to expect a high level of acoustic fidelity in the areas of musical recording and playback. By the end of the decade, stereophonic and hi-fi sound, 7-inch singles and 12-inch long-players (LPs), high-output transistor amplification and sophisticated loudspeaker design were all available to become part of the disco environment.

In Western societies, gatherings for the purpose of social dancing have a long history. While the origins of disco may be found in the context of the austerities and prohibitions imposed on wartime Paris by its German conquerors, in the United States social dancing to mediated music dates back to the 1930s when, following the repeal of Prohibition on 5 January 1933 many bars, taverns, and similar establishments reopened, now featuring jukeboxes.[22] Jukebox technology had existed since 1899, but, mainly due to severe technological drawbacks, had not seen widespread use for the next three decades. It wasn't until electric amplification, developed in the late 1920s, enabled the jukeboxes to cut through the din of social dancing environments (where earlier popular technologies such as the Victrola and the "player piano" had fallen short) that the jukebox experienced a significant rise in popularity. Starting in the 1930s, this appeal continues to the present day, even if its exclusive use for dancing has largely been discontinued. Still, as a precursor of the discotheque, the jukebox was an important factor both in the emerging American music industry and the shaping of the acoustic habits and aesthetic sensibilities of the public. The most notable consequence of the history of the jukebox is that, in the Western hemisphere, after World War II, the idea of social dancing to technologically mediated music was quite familiar.

Social dancing in New York: The gay factor

Before the disco environment became appropriated—and, in the process, transformed—by mainstream America in the mid-1970s, it was largely developed during what could be termed a laboratory phase in urban gay America. As a musical genre, disco was "an African American creation refined and popularized by DJs at underground clubs for black gay men in the late 1960s."[23] Around 1970 it crossed over to white gay male clubs, and became a mainstream phenomenon by around 1974. The resulting economic boom for the national music industry during the period 1975–80 was followed by a rapid decline, resulting in a near-total collapse of the disco industry.[24]

While the first-ever gay disco in New York State was probably in Cherry Grove on Fire Island,[25] the first urban venue that made disco rhyme with homo was the Sanctuary on West Forty-third Street. Featured in Alan Pakula's 1971 film *Klute*, it became the model for later underground gay discos such as Crisco Disco and the Tenth Floor. In hindsight, the period 1969–71 can be seen as a turning point for disco in which dancing among gay men (and those who enjoyed their company) became important to forming a community and a collective identity. In that process, the New York disco gave birth to the DJ as new type of pop star. This star played a new instrument, two turntables and a mixer, on a new stage: the DJ booth with its controls of sound and light, together with the adjacent floor addressed by a sound system putting forth nonstop, wall-to-wall sound, established the disco as a new performance environment.

By 1973, this format had so grown in popularity that disco was noted as a new trend in *Billboard* and *Rolling Stone* magazines. The next year, *Billboard* began printing DJ lists, while New York radio station WPIX was the first to air a Saturday-night "disco"/dance music show. Soon thereafter, WBLS integrated disco hits into its playlist and forced competing stations to follow suit.[26] Disco historian Brian Chin notes that "the TV show *Soul Train* provided immediate national exposure for records and instantly broadcast new dance styles all over the country. And disco-goers who didn't hear enough of the music on the radio, bought tens of thousands in the New York area alone, forcing labels to pay attention to records they'd been ignoring.[27] . . . The year 1974 was the watershed for disco's aboveground emergence: a string of #1 pop hits put the industry on notice that clubs were discovering records that would make the whole country dance."[28] As a result, DJs began to have direct input into these records. One example was David Todd who familiarized rhythm and blues producer Van McCoy with a Latin social dance called the Hustle, which resulted in the production of an eponymous record that became a big hit for McCoy on the Original Sound record label in 1975; Todd went on to develop the disco department at RCA Records. Radcliffe Joe, *Billboard* dance editor at the time, wrote that "in 1974–75, the disco music scene was literally controlled by a handful of black artists affiliated with a small group of specialized record labels led by Motown and Philadelphia International."[29]

Indeed, the magazine *The Advocate* proclaimed 1975 "the year of disco." Both RCA and Capitol Records now had disco departments, while Atlantic and Polydor Records developed disco-specific promotion techniques. In 1976, WPIX's disco show went nightly due to popular demand. That year, *Billboard* magazine hosted its first disco convention at the Roosevelt Hotel in Manhattan. Independent promotion companies devoted to disco product emerged at that time in New York, as did West End Records and Casablanca Records, which released hugely popular records by the Village People and Donna Summer.

New York's reputation as the capital of disco was confirmed and etched into the public mind of America in 1977 with the release of the very successful and influential movie *Saturday Night Fever*. While filmed on location in Manhattan and Brooklyn and featuring veteran DJ Monty Rock III, the film is by no means intended as a documentary of the local dance scene, giving instead a skewed picture of disco dancing in musical, social and sexual terms that, for better or worse, had a long-lasting impression on American audiences. Protagonist John Travolta's character is neither gay nor black, nor musically hip. More than one Bee Gees tune serves as sonic backdrop to his disco dancing, a combination that merely confirmed what

On June 27, 1999, Manny Lehman, once a fixture at Manhattan's Vinylmania record store, returned to the city to deejay the Gay Pride '99 party at Twilo. In a booth facing the dance floor, he worked three Technics SL-1200 turntables, a Urei mixer and a CD player (not shown). *Photo by the author.*

disco's detractors already knew and, after the movie's smash success, vociferously expressed: "Disco sucks!." Many disco aficionados, on the other hand, dismissed the film, and its soundtrack, altogether as a cleverly executed business venture. Indeed, by the mid-1970s, disco in general had become not only a multimillion-dollar business, but also the most prominent symbol of gay male community.[30]

Mass phenomena such as *Saturday Night Fever* and Studio 54 came in 1977, at a time when the innovative aspect of disco had peaked.[31] By then, disco had become more than the sum of its parts. After crossing over and emerging as the most popular musical style of the decade, the word itself became synonymous with a style—some say a lifestyle—that included music, dancing, fashions, hair, sex, drugs, and attitude. Moreover, the label disco was used to market everything and anything, which in turn alienated many of its original fans whose main interest had been and continued to be in its main components: music and dancing. In the words of Donna Summer's producer, Giorgio Moroder, "disco killed itself . . . too many products, too many people, too many records jumping on this kind of music. A lot of bad records came out. I guess it was overkill. Everybody started to come out with disco and it became . . . what's the word? A cussword."[32]

By 1983, disco music had returned to the gay underground. In the industry, the word disco, considered taboo, was replaced with the label dance music. According to Brian Chin, "disco had come full circle, from being ignored to being acknowledged to ignored by the industry again—all the while selling plenty of records to people who still liked to dance on weekends."[33]

Although from a 1990s' vantage point, disco is largely a historical phenomenon, an understanding of its link to today's dance music is vital. It is from the disco environment that the impulses for contemporary dance club concepts emanate, including the notion of the DJ as artist and culture hero, experimenting with and testing a new musical and dance vocabulary. By the late 1980s, the sociocultural base that laid the groundwork for the disco boom had not only aged in years, it had eroded significantly with the spread of the AIDS epidemic, a concomitant increase in homophobia, and the large-scale phasing-out of vinyl product in favor of CDs by the major recording companies. I shall return to these issues in subsequent chapters.

In contrast to *Saturday Night Fever*, two more recent, but lesser known documentary films have done more to capture and explain the connection among the dance music, gay sensibilities, and the city of New York: Leaphart's 1991 *What Is House?* and Livingston's 1990 *Paris Is Burning*. However partial and filtered in focus, an impression emerges through these films of the nonmusical contextual fabric shaped by the overlap of African American and gay expressive cultural styles. This fabric is represented by the networks of typical participants and institutions: DJs, dancers, promoters, record industry personnel, clubs, pools, recording studios, record shops. How these networks cohere, how they conceive of themselves, and how each impacts upon the nature of the music and the dance are questions not explicitly addressed by the respective filmmakers. Still, these elements—all based on the disco concept—combine to form what participants know and refer to as the underground, that is, underground music and dancing.

SIDE B

★

THREE

The Cult and Culture of the DJ[1]

"Last Night A DJ Saved My Life."[2]
—Indeep, Prelude Records, 1982

"God is a DJ."
—Faithless, Arista Records, 1998

The club DJ is a musical figure with relatively recent prominence. His (rarely her)[3] gradual rise in the hierarchy of the music industry has not been accompanied by a corresponding growth in the academic literature. As a group of musicians, cultural brokers and trendsetters, DJs in general have rarely been the topic of in-depth studies. Generally understood and referred to as protagonists of musical environments such as discotheques and dance clubs as well as radio broadcasting, the various roles as innovator, performer, musician, artist, and authority figure have not been sufficiently explored and studied. Of concern here is what makes a DJ a performer in a club setting, and to probe how exactly club DJs perform.

A comprehensive study of club DJs as performing musicians must include an examination of their performance environment. The work of a DJ cannot be explained without its relationship to the dancer. DJ and dancers in the world of UDM are interdependent performers, and their view of each other figures prominently in how DJs and dancers view themselves as performers.

Vinyl records as mediated music

The performance of UDM takes place in a setting in which a club DJ creates a musical program based on the use of prerecorded sound and music on vinyl discs. This type of performance combines aspects of musical immediacy and musical mediation, as defined and discussed earlier. While the sound on records is fixed, the DJ has a variety of means to manipulate that sound in creative ways so as to render his or her performance unique to time and place. Among the creative choices and variables are the musical repertoire; the technology used to play music for dancing; the techniques used to play, mix, and remix records into one musical performance; and the rapport and interaction between DJ and dancers. To deejay is to make mediated music immediate, using recordings, turntables, mixers, and sound reinforcement technology originally designed for recording and playback purposes only in creative ways. To understand UDM it is necessary to understand that DJs work creatively, that is, as musicians themselves, and it is also necessary to understand the forms that creativity takes. To understand underground DJs as musicians, it is not only necessary to discuss their craft and their musical equipment, but also their approach to musical artistry. This chapter focuses on the domain of the DJ.

The use of records as sound sources of music for social dancing has had a relatively short history. In ethnomusicology, for example, recordings have come to be regarded as part of a performance context only recently. Generally, the emphasis has been on their capacity to store musical information, and to serve as the basis for musical transcription and analysis. "Recordings may have been the single most important factor in getting this discipline of ethnomusicology started, freezing musical processes as objects of study, a precondition and a continuing, if largely taken for granted, frame of reference."[4]

In the context of UDM, recordings are the basis for creative individual musical expression. They are as indispensable to the DJ and his musical instruments—turntables, mixers,[5] equalizers—as strings are to violinists and guitarists and their instruments. Underlying this approach to using records creatively is what I call "the disco concept." This concept fuses mediated music and musical immediacy for the purpose of a musical performance in which a DJ interacts with a body of dancers at a specific location for a specific amount of time. To be part of a performance of this type is to be part of a musical event that, from the DJ's perspective, translates into "playing" or "spinning," and, from the dancer's perspective, is central to "clubbing." Another term for this musical environment is "the disco experience."[6]

The disco concept: Mediated music and musical immediacy

The type of musical mediation I am concerned with here is based on gramophone technology as invented by Edison and Berliner. This technology, while undergoing continued development and refinement, became so popular in the post–World War II era that the terms "recording" and "record" became associated with the gramophone technology itself. To this day, in spite of the development of other means of recording and reproducing sound, such as the magnetic tape recorder, the compact cassette, and later, digital recording technology, records are still frequently thought to be flat objects made of vinyl (in earlier times, shellac) containing sound information encoded in one tiny continuous groove that begins at the outer edge of the record and spirals slowly toward its center.[7]

This encoded sound information can only be made audible with suitable playback and amplification equipment, for which, most typically, the terms *gramophone/record player/turntable* and *amplifier/loudspeaker* have come to be used. The individual elements of this chain of sound signal processing—record, turntable, amplifier, loudspeaker—can be seen as one unit from the point of view of its operator. In this sense, a contemporary home stereo set is essentially no different from the equipment found in a discotheque, although the actual equipment, and particularly its modes of operation, may vary widely.

In the following, I shall examine how, in the context of the discotheque, playback equipment becomes a musical instrument capable of both musical mediation (by virtue of its technical design), and of musical immediacy (through the input of a DJ). The former aspect is the basis for what I call the "disco concept"; the latter pertains to what is known as "the art of spinning." The disco concept emerges from the historical conditions and consequences of the incorporation of mediated music into the context of social dancing. The discussion of the art of spinning involves contemporary application of the disco concept by DJs in underground clubs of disco's capital, New York City.

The art of spinning: The DJ as musician

Can spinning records be considered an art form, as part of an artworld? Because turntables and vinyl recordings were, until recently, mass consumer goods, why should playing records be considered something special? What are the musical skills of a DJ, and what exactly is his musical instrument? How does a DJ make "his" music, using prerecorded sound? And how has this approach to making music by DJs developed over time? Because a DJ thinks of his musical personality as something that is determined by *how* he mixes as much as *what* he mixes, issues of technique and technology versus repertoire will be treated separately.

DJ technology

The general notion of a DJ is that of a person who operates a turntable. Whether a radio DJ, a club DJ or a mobile DJ who travels with a mobile sound system to accommodate his audiences at weddings or birthday parties, all three play records to entertain or otherwise engage an audience.[8] The basic necessities for a DJ, therefore, are his records and the equipment to make them audible to an audience. Modern-day club DJs typically use two turntables, a mixer, and two separate amplification systems to address the dance floor and the DJ booth. Depending on the sophistication of the P.A. system, a crossover or another equalization unit may also be available. Once the amplification system is set to the DJ's liking, his main instruments for the evening are the twin turntable and the mixer. These three form one unit that sometimes is referred to as the "console" or "set."

The turntables are usually installed so that vibrations from the floor or the P.A. system don't affect the playback mode; typically, the mixer is installed between or in front of the turntables for easy access. While mixers vary greatly in design, features, and mode of operation, turntable technology has hardly changed since the mid-1980s. Versions of one heavy-duty Technics turntable model (the SL-1200) are installed in most DJ booths in New York dance venues, DJ record stores, and record pools, having become an industry standard since their introduction in the early 1980s.[9] This standard has affected DJ technique, to the extent that the art of spinning is practiced on basically one type of turntable, which features a high-torque, direct-drive motor and vari-speed control.

Two Technics, a mixer and some headphones. The standard set-up for a club DJ consists of at least two turntables, a mixer (preferably Technics SL-1200 and a Urei respectively, as shown here), and a pair of headphones. A Crown power amp (lower left), a graphic equalizer (above the mixer), and a pair of loudspeakers (not shown) complete the picture. *Photo by the author.*

DJ technique

From the perspective of the general public, the technique of spinning appears too similar to playing records to be considered anything but fairly straightforward. This may be one of the reasons why deejaying is sometimes not viewed as a very prestigious activity or profession: it is not readily associated with the specific musical skills or technique traditional musicians must acquire.

This perspective changes once one considers the twin turntable set and the mixer as one instrument consisting of three units that have to be operated simultaneously as well as synchronously in order to allow the art of spinning to emerge. The coordination of two turntables and a mixer requires intimate knowledge of the appliances and operation skills that can be acquired only through practice. The extent of this knowledge is most apparent whenever a DJ segues from one song to another, which necessitates switching from one turntable to the other by using the mixer to control the audio signal flow and balance. At that time, the simultaneous control of tempo, volume, and balance of timbres and textures is crucial. The tempo of the music depends on the speed of the turntable which, on a Technics SL 1200, is adjustable from –8 percent to +8 percent. Many DJs, especially the older vanguard, developed their speed control skills on turntables other than the SL 1200, and have stuck to the techniques that work on belt-driven units or those without a built-in speed control. Accordingly, slowing down is accomplished by touching the rotating platter with a thumb or finger applying the desired amount of friction, whereas an index finger applied toward the outer edge of the record's center label is used to speed up the tempo, usually to get it in sync with the record on the other turntable.

Among club DJs, the most common way of segueing from one record to the next is by slip-cuing. Other techniques are fast "cuts" and "overlays." Fast cutting involves the rapid, almost instantaneous switch between turntables, usually just before the first downbeat of the section or song about to be played. Overlays are achieved by playing two records at the same time through the P.A. system for an extended period of time, often lasting minutes. The aim here is to synchronize two different records so as to make them sound like one piece of music.

When using two copies of the same record, other effects can be obtained with the same setup. When started at the same time, the two records will still be slightly out of phase with each other, producing a sound referred to as "phasing." Alternatively, one turntable can act as a shadow of the other, producing an echo effect. Some DJs have gone as far as experimenting with tone arms mounted upside down, which can play a record backward from below if the record is mounted on a spindle that lifts it high enough from the platter. "Transforming" is yet another technique, used primarily by hip-hop DJs to produce a stuttering effect in sync with the metric subdivisions of the music. The two techniques mentioned last are hardly ever encountered in the context of UDM, however, where programming is often prioritized over the technical aspects of spinning. DJ Tony Humphries who has worked professionally since 1977 and has been a major influence on his peers in New York City, speaks from an underground perspective:

DJs have to understand the concept of programming. How to break a record. How to play with records, repeat intros, lengthen breaks, endings. . . . There is an art to programming. . . . The DJ who plays all his hottest records in a row is not doing his job right. You can't play all your best material at once because you want to save some of it for later in the evening. The DJ doesn't get into that power record the same way that the crowd does. You're supposed to be separate from the crowd. You're supposed to be into exposing them to newer material. So, what you do is you play a track, followed by something new and then you back it up with something that they know and like. It's like a train ride. The clubgoers become very trustworthy that you will come back with something they like. It's the 15-minute game. About every third song, you give them a well-known song. After one hour, the crowd has been exposed to ten new records. That way, you please yourself as well as the crowd. Larry Levan was great at this. The most important thing to remember is that musical content, i.e. how you program, is more important than actual mixing skills.[10]

DJ repertoire: Programming versus mixing

Someone who has mastered the operation of two, or even three turntables and a mixer is thus not necessarily a good DJ. Paradise Garage DJ Larry Levan, praised in the preceding quote, explained his approach in a 1983 interview: "When I listen to DJs today they don't mean anything to me. Technically some of them are excellent—emotionally they can't do anything for me. . . . There is actually a message in the dance, the way you feel, the muscles you use, but only certain records have that."[11] These "certain records" and how they are employed are the ultimate indications of a DJ's quality, skill, and style, as the preceding comments show. A DJ's technical skill is thus at best equal to his choices in repertoire.

Club DJ technology is usually stationary; looking similar to the cockpit of an airplane, the DJ booth is the command center of the venue's sound system, complete with units controlling the lighting and other special effects such as smoke and fog machines, possibly video screens and definitely a sound system with enough wattage to power outdoor events. The DJ's repertoire—his music—however, travels with the DJ. While some clubs have a (usually limited) record library, most underground DJs bring several crates of records to each venue where they play. These crates are then stacked in the DJ booth, often facing the set so that the DJ positions himself between the set and the records. Whereas hip-hop DJs may employ a helper to help handle and store records as they are switched at a quick pace, underground DJs usually do the programming by themselves. For efficiency's sake, the records are organized according to the DJ's own criteria, and intimate familiarity with this organization and the records themselves are considered essential to efficient deejaying. There is no standard way of organizing records, however. The most common categories are new as opposed to old records, the latter often being referred to as "classics." In addition, DJs differentiate between the stylistic categories of house, acid house, deep house, techno, trance, vocals, instrumentals or tracks, acapellas, and sound effects. Some arrange their records by label, and distinguish between major and indie label releases, as well as between domestic and import records. According to my observations, not one DJ uses bpm (beats per minute) as an organizational principle.

Whenever a club DJ arrives for work, he brings his music, his records, with him. If not packed into cases built by one of the companies specializing in DJ equipment, they will typically be stacked in milk crates, holding about sixty records each. Depending on the design of the booth, these cases or crates are then stacked side by side to give the DJ the easiest access while he is operating the console. In most cases this involves placing the records behind the DJ or to the side(s) of the console. DJ David Depino comments on repertoire programming and mixing:

[Through] shopping at all different stores and shopping often you find things that make you different [from] everybody else. And that's the magic. I don't go to any other clubs, because I don't want to hear what other DJs are playing. . . . Every DJ out there mixes well, . . . nobody can't mix. It's personal taste, what you play and when you play it. . . . [So] you're coming to me to hear what I like; what I'm turning you on to. So there's got to be some difference [between DJs]. I believe that, or else then there's no need to have more than one club in New York. . . . My club [Tracks] is open from ten to four, and nobody even gets there until twelve, one o'clock, and they're gone before four, [so] I've got three, four hours to really let people hear good music—my taste in music, and what they want to hear. Junior [Vasquez, then the resident DJ at Sound Factory] is open from twelve to twelve, he's got twelve hours to do it. I got four hours. . . . I can't go through many different moods like I used to. Tracks used to be open at 9:00 [P.M.], crowded by 9:30, and I used to close at 7:00 [A.M.]. I had many hours. I could have took them through an oldies hour or two, I could have took them downtempo, uptempo, mood swings, unusual music. [I] can't do it right now.[12]

Sound Factory DJ Junior Vasquez echoes DePino's concerns, placing programming above mixing skills:

"Someone just bought it." Four examples of DJ specialty retail in New York. Although specializing in 12-inch vinyl singles, these stores also sell CDs to a clientele consisting largely of DJs, both amateur and professional. Shown clockwise from the top are Vinylmania Records on Carmine Street, Eightball Records/The Shop on East 9th Street, Downtown Records on West 28th Street, and Disc-O-Rama on West 4th Street. *Photos by the author.*

I'm in partnership with the other owners of my club, so I can . . . play whatever I like. In theory I could play music that clears my dance floor and not have to worry about getting replaced next week. . . . What's too bad is that with the recent harassment of dance clubs by city agencies, it gets harder and harder to create the kind of club I really want. I have always relied upon having a 10- to 12-hour night in which to play everything I think is important. A long night allows a jock to completely satisfy at least two different kinds of club goers. The crowd who dances to you at 6:00 or 7:00 A.M. is pretty much ready for you to lead them wherever you will, which is a very powerful position for a jock to be in. My 4:00 A.M.-to-noon crowd could let me know which records the 10:00 P.M.-to-4:00 crowd would like three months down the line. If I have to force those two crowds to party together, I run the risk of pleasing no one—including myself.[13]

Doug Shannon, a former DJ from Cleveland, who includes a discussion of DJ mixing skills in his book chapter "The Art Of Programming," associates mixing with skills versus programming with art when he says that "mixing can be considered one link in the entire chain of programming."[14] These hierarchical associations essentially reflect the priorities agreed upon earlier by Humphries, DePino, and Vasquez. Programming also goes beyond mixing since it recognizes the dynamic interaction between two different energy levels, one sonic, the other kinetic, and understands both as constantly changing entities. Programming is an art that can include a range of musical considerations. On one end of that spectrum is the musical moment, the instant a certain sound travels from the needle following the record's groove to the eardrums of the dancer. On the other end, programming can consider the overall duration of a night of uninterrupted music for dancing with its slow and gradual increase of energy at the beginning, the pacing toward one or several peaks that find their ultimate release in that last record, followed by the silence that signals the arrival of, the return to, another day, a different and new reality.

Peaking the floor

DJs aim to prompt as strong as possible a response from the floor at least once during the evening. When successful, these moments manifest themselves as peaks. Both DJs and dancers are aware of the significance of the moments, as the ultimate manifestation of the communication linking the booth with the floor.

Miezitis explains this type of moment as "a peak of excitement, and energy when the music is most stimulating, when the crowd is the largest and the most loosened up, most energetic, and when the lights and theatrics resemble a grand stage finale. The peak is like a sexual climax when everything and everyone flows together, a moment when time seems erased."[15] Harvey observed this kind of energy at Paradise Garage: "an awesome

Frankie Knuckles cues up a record in the booth at Sound Factory Bar in Manhattan. At his request, the DJ booth of this downtown venue was moved from the second floor to a location adjacent to the dance floor, as shown in this picture. *Photo © Tina Paul, 1989.*

sound system continuously expounding the most serious black music and an audience of thousands of dancers whose interconnected energy makes the main dance room feel like a rocket at the point of lift-off."[16] During his long shifts at Sound Factory, Junior Vasquez felt "the night achieves several peaks—one at five, another at eight, and maybe even a 'fluffy-muscle-queen peak' later on."[17] For Frankie Knuckles, the experience of peaking the floor makes the club feel "like church."[18] The following excerpt from an interview published in *Dance Music Report* shows that the intensity of the dance floor quickly affects the booth as well. It also exemplifies a DJ's focus and concentration on the dancers' collective energy:

REYNOLDS: When you get your crowd up to a peak, what's that like for you up in the booth?
KNUCKLES: It's crazy. I never really get a chance to focus in on it because when I do get the room going like that there's like a ton of people that try to rush the booth at the same time. It breaks my concentration up. . . . And I'm not just talking about people that are hanging out. I mean industry people. They have to be in that booth and they always have something . . . to say while I'm trying really, to feed off that energy that's coming back from everybody on the dance floor. When the room starts taking off, I don't know, I guess a lot of people feel that they need to be right there. . . . I think they feel the need to be in that booth where all that energy is coming from.[19]

Beyond mixing: The DJ as cultural hero

Goldman has described how through the influence of early discotheque DJs in New York such as Terry Noel (at Arthur and Salvation) and Francis Grasso (at Salvation and Sanctuary), the art of spinning, originally developed in discotheques in Paris, France, was gradually transformed into a new form of American vernacular art: the art of mixing.[20] In the 1970s, the emergence of disco as a mainstream phenomenon owes as much to the creativity of people like Francis Grasso as to the development of new technology (of primary concern to DJs). Two important developments were the 12-inch record and the direct-drive turntable with speed control. Prior to these innovations, the technology of musical mediation in discotheques, with the exception of the amplification system, was close to the technology marketed toward the general consumer of recorded music. Records came in two formats agreed upon, after a battle for market shares, by the competitors RCA and Columbia. Whereas the 12-inch 33⅓ rpm LP was regarded as the more "serious" format, the 7-inch 45 rpm single ruled for many years in the pop domain despite its technical shortcomings when compared to the LP.[21]

In addition of the standardized formats and conventions of an industry concerned primarily with pop product, early disco DJs had to deal with the particularities of the standard playback equipment, especially with the inconsistencies of belt-driven turntables. When switched on, a belt-driven turntable requires a significant amount of time before it reaches either of the two fixed speeds (33⅓ or 45 rpm). With the addition of speed controls at both 33⅓ and 45 rpm and the option of controlling the rotation speed directly via a quartz-controlled motor instead of indirectly via a rubber belt, mixing has become less laborious and more flexible. Even if it is now possible to adjust two records so as to play in sync with each other, it still takes manual dexterity and skill to slow down or speed up a spinning record without noticeable pitch or tempo changes (liable to annoy or confuse the dancers).

As described above, slip-cuing is one way of stitching together song after song, into one endless, uninterrupted flow of music. Pieces of songs can be superimposed over one another, creating a new musical effect and affect at the same time. Through creatively exploiting the means of playback technology, each DJ has acquired the means to become a musical author, producing his own interpretations of prerecorded music, not only though the choice of his repertoire, but also through his style of mixing. In New York, this concept, formulated by DJs such as Terry Noel and Francis Grasso, continued with such influential figures as David Mancuso (at the Loft), Nicky Siano (at the Gallery) and Larry Levan (at the Paradise Garage), up to a generation of younger DJs of the 1980s and 1990s in an unbroken tradition.[22] Almost half a century after the first discotheque, this tradition still has no textbook or manual, no comprehensive documentation, and no established recognition as a form of musical artistry. Rather, it is carried orally, by DJs and dancers who learned from those who came before them.[23]

Part of the relative obscurity of this unbroken tradition can be explained by the fact that it developed largely out of sight of the public eye, in the dance underground of the city. It was not until rap music broke into the mass media in 1979 that the concept of a DJ as an artist and culture hero gradually became formulated.[24] As dance or party music, rap had developed at the same time as disco, but with a different sociocultural territory and agenda.[25] Whereas the name for this musical genre prioritizes its verbal component, historically the central musician in rap has been the DJ, respected as the "master on the wheels of steel."

On the surface, the ascendance of the DJ is a result of rap's pervasiveness. More significantly, the . . . DJ stands at a cultural crossroads—the post-modern intersection of "high" art and "low" folk traditions. By using an everyday appliance to make sound collages that people can dance to, the DJ signifies the fusion of avant-garde and entertainment. [He descends], on the one hand, from John Cage's "Imaginary Landscape," a 1939 percussion piece whose instrumentation included two phonographs; on the other, from Grandmaster Flash, whose 1981 audio collage, "The Adventures of Grandmaster Flash on the Wheels of Steel" stands alongside Jimi Hendrix's abstract-expressionist "Star-Spangled Banner" as one of pop music's most dazzling moments.[26]

The hip-hop DJs who ventured into the institutions of the entertainment industry (primarily recording as well as radio and television broadcast studios) were actually preceded by disco DJs. By the time Harvey published his survey of the New York "disco underground," its protagonists weren't merely DJs anymore. They had acquired a new title, "mixer," which, by the end of the decade, changed from mixer to remixer and remixer/producer.[27]

The need to mix originally arose from the limitations of early DJ technology. With only one turntable to play records for dancing, there would be "dead" time between each record, disrupting the continuous dynamics of a dance floor atmosphere. Dead time could be avoided by using two turntables, but their outputs had to be fed through the same sound system.[28] Hence the need for a device to alternate between the audio signals from two (or more) turntables. This device, the mixer, originally evolved in the context of multitrack recording technology. A mixer, known as the "board" or "console" allows for control of all audio aspects of individual sound sources.[29] It can therefore be used for both recording and playback purposes.

Whereas mixers in modern recording studios are gigantic devices, featuring up to forty-eight channels, a DJ mixer is typically small, portable, and, in many instances allows for often no more than four to six inputs, as is the case of the rack mount Urei 1620 mixer (which has become a DJ standard among mixers almost to the same extent that Technics SL-1200 turntables have). However, in the hands of an adept DJ, the turntables and the mixer become one instrument that in turn becomes the vehicle for a musical performance

This view of the record distribution room at For The Record shows the bins from which the 100 members pick up their records regularly. The pool, one of the oldest in New York and run by Judy Weinstein, shares office space with Def Mix Productions, a remix/ production company matching remix talent, including Grammy award-winning DJs Frankie Knuckles and David Morales, to major recording companies. *Photo by the author.*

DJ repertoire. Labeled either EP or mini-album, every one of these four records, released on independent record labels between 1988 and 1999, exemplifies underground dance music. Shown clockwise from top left are The Black Cuban Opera's *Symphonies from the Underground* (Black China Records); DJ Work!'s *Work-Is-Abstract EP* (Underground Construction Music/Strictly Hype Recordings); the compilation Underground *Dance Music Volume 1* (Big Beat Records); and the hard-to-find *Back-To-Basics* mini-album by the Black Rascals (New York Underground). *Clockwise from top left: two photos © Saskia Fikentscher, 1999; photo © Alex Smith, 1999; photo © Saskia Fikentscher, 1999.*

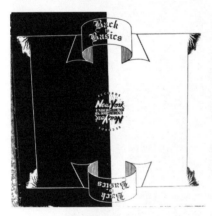

in which the elements of timbre, tempo, and texture, of balance of sound and volume, combine to an artistic and aesthetic statement. It is through the playing of this instrument that a DJ's individual style is recognized, measured, and evaluated. By using a device called a "mixer," New York DJs in the late 1960s and 1970s transformed the art of spinning into the art of mixing, and in the process became known themselves as mixers.

During the 1970s and 1980s, many DJs became record producers by involving themselves in the recording process as the flip side of their normal activities, which involved primarily the manipulation of musical sound in

The song does not remain the same. Both the interrogative (Can you feel it?) and the affirmative (I can feel it) forms appear numerous times as titles for distinct house records. The four examples pictured here are, clockwise from top left, by CLS (both the domestic release on Strictly Rhythm Records, 1991, and the double 12-inch import from Italy on UMM Records, 1992); by Mr. Fingers (Trax Records, 1986); and by Chez Damier (KMS Records, 1992). *Clockwise from top left: three photos © Saskia Fikentscher, 1999; photo © Alex Smith, 1999.*

the process of playback. The additional involvement meant a transfer of sound manipulation into the realm of recording and caused a blurring of the conceptual divisions among production and reproduction, sound engineer, producer, and DJ. It started a new industry within the American music business: the dance music industry.[30] Its characteristic institutions are the record pool and the DJ specialty retail store, and its central format is the 12-inch single. Straw, while discussing pools at some length, does little to recognize the importance of the 12-inch as a innovative industry format. The most influential figure in this context is Tom Moulton, a New York DJ turned producer who conceived the 12-inch single, thereby setting what has become the standard sound carrier format of the dance music industry.[31]

While the development of the 12-inch single has been detailed elsewhere,[32] it is important to note that Moulton's inception of the 12-inch single as the ideal disco format coincided with the first establishment (by David Mancuso) of a record pool in New York. Two entities that were to become characteristic of the as yet nonexistent dance music industry emerged almost simultaneously, at the time when local radio disc-jockeys began to accept club DJs as trendsetters by playing what they had heard in the clubs.[33] There would have been no disco boom in 1975 without the coincidence of these three crucial developments; indeed disco would not have grown into a multimillion-dollar enterprise without them.

The rise of the club DJ: Remix and production work

The emergence of the 12-inch format has been explained as "the only logical alternative . . . for record companies to place longer versions on special promotional album-size . . . records. These . . . would enable longer cuts and a different studio mix to be used, compared to what was available on an album or 45 and would also assure that a song's reproduction would . . . have better sound quality and greater volume."[34] These concerns reflect a compromise between what DJs wanted record companies to provide them with, and what advantages and risks record companies saw in terms of marketing. Only "after the longer cuts . . . on promotional 12-inch singles began to increase in numbers and in popularity through discotheque exposure, did record companies realize there was a potential commercial market for 12-inch singles."[35] They subsequently started to issue 12-inch singles for commercial release in the fall of 1976. To differentiate the new format, 12-inch singles were marketed as "Giant 45" or "Giant Single." This was supposed to underscore their nature as singles, and to avoid confusion with the similar-looking album, for which 12-inch singles quickly came to serve as a promotional tool. The packaging was also different. From the beginning, many 12-inch singles were (and still are) most often dressed in a plain one-color record jacket with the center cut out to show the sticker bearing the song titles on the record.

Initially, then, early 12-inch records contained extended versions of songs that, in most cases, were also available in shorter form on 45s or LPs, with the B-side often providing the same music without vocals. This latter version was called "instrumental" or "instrumental version," even if remnants of the voicetrack were present. Over time, the term "mix" became used synonymously with "version," and eventually the former term displaced the latter, both in usage and in print on vinyl records and record jackets. Thus, a term used primarily in the recording studio became adopted in the environment of the discotheque or club as well.

In the former context, a mix denotes the phase following a stage of multitrack recording, or the product of that phase, during which the final balance of all tracks to each other in terms of volume and timbre is determined. In that sense, a mix is comparable to a score in the context of Western art music: an authoritative text. In the context of a dance venue, however, a mix refers to the blending, by a DJ, of records and, perhaps, sound effects, accomplished with less sophisticated equipment and in real time. A DJ's performance then actually constitutes a "remix," as he uses, for his own mix, vinyl recordings that have been previously mixed in the recording studio.

Roger Sanchez has recourse to a bank of samplers in his basement home studio. Having just loaded a sample from a Vestax turntable (see photo that follows), he now edits it to fit into a layer of other samples already loaded into his sequencer. *Photo by the author.*

Another angle of Roger Sanchez' sample station. Shown from front to back are a Vestax turntable, a Emu SL-1200 sampler/sequencer, a master keyboard and a computer loaded with hard disk recording and sequencing software. *Photo by the author.*

In the course of the 1980s, however, particularly with the advent of sampling technology, remixing made its way into the recording studio, this time as a money-intensive industry. Not only were musical sections stretched, through the repetition of material already available on the recording masters, but individual tracks were redone, either by using different signal processing technology (for example, echo, different equalization) or by actual rerecording using additional musicians (often the same as, or recruited from, the production team).[36] The results of this approach became known as *remixes*, to differentiate them from the "original" mixes found on 45s, LPs, or previously released 12-inch singles. DJs who use remixes for their "live"-mixes at dance venues only add another layer to the remix concept. Musical authorship has become a temporary and subjective issue.

A DJ's home studio in working mode. Two digital Yamaha mixers, a patch bay, and a pair of reference monitors form the control center of Roger Sanchez' home studio. *Photo by the author.*

The early 1980s were a period in which the lines between studio producers, engineers, songwriters, and DJs became increasingly fuzzy. Many DJs, in addition to spinning records at clubs, ventured into dance music production, bringing many of the workplace concepts and techniques into the recording studio. In the process, the art of mixing using a multitrack console and recorder, and of mixing at a dance venue, using two or more turntables and a comparatively unsophisticated audio mixer, began to converge. The more savvy DJs were the first to feed the know-how thus acquired back to the dance venue. As a result, the number of versions found on a 12-inch single increased from two (A- and B-side) to about four to six. To account for this expansion, different categories of versions or mixes were developed during this period, as DJs became increasingly involved in the songwriting, producing, and engineering of dance music.

The oldest of these now more or less standard categories is the dub. Its roots are in the DJ culture of 1960s Jamaica, associated with mobile sound systems and associated competitive teams of DJs. Outstanding traits of the original dub, which has evolved into a sub-genre of 1970s reggae, is the treatment of song structure and the addition of sound effects, notably echo. Through the use of two copies of the same record, sections can be shortened or extended, the vocal part removed and substituted with "live" performances of "dub poets," "DJs" or "toasters."[37] Featured on 12-inch dance singles since the mid-1980s, dubs have become one of the main categories of remixing. For underground club DJs who have ventured into remixing, a dub is an opportunity to make individual statements as musical authors. The following excerpt from an interview with New York DJ/remixer Victor Simonelli is representative of the meaning of dub mixing for New York remixers.

SIMONELLI: Now a dub gets fun, like I can experiment a lot. A dub mix is fun, because I'm able to do whatever I want.
FIKENTSCHER: As in "Do your thing?" "Go crazy?"
SIMONELLI: Oh yeah. A dub is "do your thing." Arrangement doesn't really make a difference. It's just a "feel" thing, mainly. It's different in each situation, but I'm talking about most of the time.
FIKENTSCHER: Some people equate dubs with instrumentals.
SIMONELLI: Sure. Like, let's say . . . I mean, definitely. I agree with that.
FIKENTSCHER: Okay. Although some records have instrumental versions.
SIMONELLI: And also a dub version. And the difference between an instrumental [and a] dub could be a lot of delay, or vocals coming in an out, breakdowns that you wouldn't expect, just interesting stuff like surprises you. No standard format. There is no standard format to a dub in my opinion, or I never found one.
FIKENTSCHER: Dub is a fun environment for you.
SIMONELLI: Right.
FIKENTSCHER: Interesting. Because Junior [Vasquez], on the other hand, gets accused of playing too many of those at the Sound Factory.
SIMONELLI (*laughs*): To tell you the truth, most of the stuff that gets played in clubs today around the city would be considered dubs. (Interview, 7 November 1992)[38]

In addition to containing one extended, one instrumental, and one or more dub mixes, 12-inch dance singles released in the late 1980s or early 1990s often feature at least one of the following:

- A "club mix," that refers to a specific dance venue, associating the mix with the type of music the venue has come to be associated with. Accordingly, mixes may refer to renowned dance venues in and around New York City, such as 10–18 (which was and again is Roxy), Paradise Garage, Shelter, Sound Factory, Twilo, or Zanzibar.[39]
- A mix bearing the name of the author of the version in question, in almost all cases a DJ. Some examples are Larry Levan, Shep Pettibone, Steve Hurley, and Masters at Work, the production team formed by Louie Vega and Kenny Gonzalez.[40] This underscores the higher social status accorded to DJs who have broken into the remix business.
- A mix named after a specific category of dance music, such as house, deep house, techno, hip-hop, tribal, or rave.[41]
- One of either an "acapella" or "percapella" mix. Acapella refers to the vocal track of a master only, while percapella, the contraction of the words "percussion" and "acapella," indicates the presence of some, usually light, percussion.

- A "radio edit," also called "7-inch edit," which represents a mix whose duration and arrangement conforms with standards used in radio programming, and is often identical with the album and/or 7-inch single version.
- A "bonus track" (*track* here refers to one cut on a vinyl record). If called "bonus beats," this is a version stripped of all instrumentation except the percussion and, perhaps, a bass line. The less frequent alternative is to include a bonus track consisting of an entirely different song, in the way that some CDs feature songs that are not included on albums featuring otherwise identical music and packaging.

These categories of mixes are the result of a gradual process during which DJs became key players in a new type of music industry. This industry is now built upon the concept of remixing as recycling one musical piece in as many appearances as feasible, in order to target a variety of markets distinguished by musical style. It took about a decade for this concept and industry to develop. Initially, DJs such as Vasquez and Simonelli were hired to do "edits"; that is, to extend the song, particularly introductions, breaks, and instrumental sections, for 12-inch versions. They did not otherwise tamper with them. "It was a triumph when you could add a conga," recalls *Billboard*'s dance music editor Larry Flick.[42] However, remixing became established not on its artistic, innovative, or aesthetic merits, but for economic considerations.[43] Writing for the *New York Times* in 1992, Rob Tannenbaum quotes Leslie Doyle, at the time national director of dance music at Elektra Records: "'Remixers can salvage records.' For just a few thousand dollars . . . , these audio auteurs refashion records to match changing styles. Success has made the practice rampant; one executive estimates that half the singles on the Top 100 chart are remixed."[44]

This estimate comes almost a decade after the practice that led to its formulation was initiated by enterprising DJs both in the fields of early house and pre–"Yo! MTV Raps"[45] hip-hop. Tannenbaum credits the evolution of remixing from underground novelty to major-label standard practice to pop artist Madonna: "Madonna, the most statistically significant artist of the '80s, carried dance music out of the underground and into the mainstream. [At that time], a cadre of remixers—mostly black and Latino, often gay, came to dominate the field, and dance-oriented acts released entire albums of remixes. Soon the job title was a misnomer: remixers were also rearranging, rewriting and reproducing."[46]

Shep Pettibone, mentioned earlier, had abandoned deejaying—both in New York clubs such as Better Days and on Kiss FM where his *Mastermix* show had an influential four-year run—by 1984 to move completely into remixing and producing. He subsequently worked as a remixer for several prominent pop singers, such as Michael Jackson and Madonna, who has gone on record expressing her preference for his remixes over her original productions.[47] After the first two collaborations with Madonna went to No. 1 on the charts, Pettibone's career was forever transformed.

The evolution from spinning to mixing to remixing to producing, as exemplified by Pettibone, has been a gradual and continuous process for most DJs who went that route. Over time, through the increasing involvement by DJs in the art of recordmaking, the transfer of technologies and aesthetics between the recording studio and the DJ booth increased to a level so financially profitable that for years it has been the driving force behind the dance music industry. As a result, representing its characteristic institutions—the independent label, the record pool, the underground club, the specialty retail store—are now a group of DJs who base their activities as remixers, producers, A&R (artist and repertoire) agents and recording artists on an ever-expanding concept of their art as musicianship.[48] In addition to enjoying the loyalty of their dance floor clienteles, these DJs wield more influence and money-earning power in the music industry than ever before. The increase in status from record spinner to record producer has transformed the club DJ from cult figure to cultural hero—even if the culture in question is still of marginal, subcultural character in the United States.

An inside look at an independent record company. Just three years old and going strong, Joe Claussell's Spiritual Life Records is located on the fourth floor of a midtown loft building on Seventh Avenue. *Photo by the author.*

Conclusion: Why 12-inch vinyl is critical

The development of the 12-inch single and its almost immediate appeal to consumers, especially to DJs, has played an enormous role in the emergence and evolution of the dance music industry in America, with New York City as its center. The picture that emerges from the rather tight connections between 12-inch vinyl technology and DJ performance technology, DJ technique (spinning, mixing) and style (programming, working, remixing) explains how both the acoustic properties of the 12-inch single as analog medium and the physicality of the equipment (records, turntables, mixers) have helped shape the art and craft of dance music performance as it developed in New York City for more than a quarter of a century. Although during this time other sound carriers were developed and mass-marketed, it is not surprising that most New York DJs, and virtually all those who work in the dance underground prefer vinyl over any other sound carrier format.

Since the late 1980s, a situation of conflicting interests within the recording industry has arisen, as digital audio carriers, most notably the CD, surpassed analog carriers such as vinyl and, to a lesser extent, cassette tape in terms of sales. Being disproportionately more profitable than vinyl, CD technology has effectively marginalized vinyl in the general music consumer market, which is dominated by major recording companies (known as "majors"). Within the dance music industry, independent companies ("indies") have attempted to fill the vinyl void created by the majors. Since the initial phasing-out of vinyl product by the majors around the turn of the decade, the number of independent labels catering exclusively to the dance music industry has increased. These companies, which initially almost exclusively dealt in vinyl product, were affected by the shrinkage in the vinyl market. Over the last few years, the number of 12-inch single sales has decreased. In response, independent label executives have turned to marketing music that may yield higher sales, such as hip-hop (Strictly Rhythm Records; Nervous Records) or techno (Radikal Records), reissued old catalog repertoire on CD (Easy Street Records; Cutting Records), or have gone out of business altogether (NuGroove Records, 111 East Records). Almost without exception, these and similar companies are now selling their catalog on both vinyl and CD.

"The vinyl record is going to be the black-and-white television set of the audio world. It will be around, but in small numbers. Just as the color TV has taken over, the CD eventually will." So judged Michael Gussick, president of Easy Street Records (personal communication, 1993). Only two years earlier, Mark Finkelstein, president of Strictly Rhythm Records, had taken a slightly more optimistic position:

Here is my take on the difference between vinyl, CDs, cassettes, and why I don't think vinyl should ever be replaced, albeit will be because it's not as profitable. To get the warmth of the sound you need an analog format. And that leaves you with vinyl and cassette. Cassette doesn't work, for two reasons: One, you can't mix cassettes, and secondly they have an inherent tape sound, tape hiss . . . the [sound of the] CD is too bright, too thin, too exact. Vinyl has got the warmth of the mechanical absorption of the sound through the vibration of the needle that you cannot otherwise replicate. You can get a depth of sound that you cannot get on CD. . . . I mean I can identify a Strictly Rhythm record that's playing in a club because I walk in there and I feel the bass in my chest. . . . As the majors pull out [of the vinyl industry], it leaves a void in the market place, and we (at Strictly Rhythm) have learned that where there is a demand, there will be a supply. So as they pull out, that DJ who is now looking for something to play Saturday night will pick up a Strictly Rhythm record.[49]

With few exceptions, almost two decades after the introduction of the CD, vinyl records remain the norm in New York underground dance clubs. Although most DJs continue to view digital audio as inappropriate for club-playing purposes,[50] some DJs have begun to use CD recorders alongside DAT machines in order to transfer rough mixes and unreleased tracks from the recording studio to the dance club or radio show.[51] Overall, however, the indications are strong that the vinyl market will be central to the dance music industry for quite some time to come.

FOUR

The Dancers
Working (It) Out

"The House of God."
—D.H.S, Hangman Records, 1991

This chapter focuses on the dancer's role in, and perspective on UDM in New York City. Based on the concept of collective performance, as defined below, the phenomenon of underground dancing is discussed in relation to the history of social dance in twentieth-century America. A discussion of the dancing body as musical instrument will be followed by an examination of the relationship of musical performance to nonmusical issues of individual and group identity and marginality. As underground club dancing may differ from one particular club or group of dancers to another in terms of structure, style, and interpretation, those factors seen as defining one group versus another are key in underground club culture. Primary among these factors are age, ethnicity, and sexual orientation. Lastly, the concept of interactive performance will be introduced to investigate the relationship between dancing and deejaying. Unfolding within a specific cultural setting as a process with specific musical traits, these two predominant concepts of UDM—mediated music made immediate through deejaying, and collective performance realized through dancing—relate to each other as simultaneous, interactive modes of performance.

Dancing: Interactive versus collective performance

Christopher Small has suggested the term *musicking* to describe any form of participation in a musical performance. He proposes to view music not only as noun, but as verb as well, in order to "express the act of taking part in a musical performance. . . . All [persons] involved in any way in a musical performance can be thought of as musicking."[1] In the context of UDM, I use the term "collective performance" in a similarly comprehensive fashion. I do this, not only in agreement with the idea of music as an activity rather than an object, but in recognition of the African American cultural context of the musical tradition both Small's and my text address (see chapter 5).

In view of UDM as an environment that is socially, culturally, and musically recognizable as part of the African American cultural stream, collective performance refers to the sum of multiple interactions between individual dancers sharing one circumscribed space. While the result of the interdependence and dynamic interaction between musicking in the DJ booth of a disco or dance club on one hand, and the musicking on the adjoining dance floor on the other could be described as collective performance as well, in the sense that both activities occur simultaneously and in relation to each other, I prefer to term the relationship between DJ and dancers "interactive" rather than collective. Underground club dancing is characterized by collective performance on the floor as much as by the interaction of this performance with that of the DJ in the booth: that is, the performance of mediated music. The environment of UDM (as with many other social dance environments) is thus one where musicking in sound and musicking in movement happen simultaneously and in relation to each other.

Particular to UDM performance is the division of labor among its participants. Typically, there are no dancing musicians, nor are there dancers who make music.[2] This division applies to the performance space as well. The musical performance in sound, as the DJ's domain, takes place in the DJ booth. The musical performance in movement, or dance, however, takes place on the floor populated by dancers. UDM is thus characterized by two key aspects, music on the sonic level, and dance on the kinetic level; each level is assigned to a specific performing force (DJ versus dancers) and performance site (booth versus floor). For UDM patrons, however, these two aspects are perceived and understood as parts that combine to create one single performance experience that is often referred to as "disco experience."[3]

In contrast to the DJ's domain, where generally one person, inside a booth set apart from the dance space, masterminds a musical performance, the dancer's domain is characterized by collectivity. Sharing the space available for dancing, the dancers perform in relation to each other, and to the DJ, as one collective entity or "body." This does not negate the individuality of each dancer. Rather, it affirms the position of the DJ as authority figure who provides the musical "call" to which the dancers collectively "respond" in dance.

As much as the DJ uses his set and his records as musical instruments, the dancers use their bodies. Musicking in the context of UDM involves the dancing body as musical instrument. Enacted on a dance floor shared by a multitude of individual bodies, collective performance has the additional potential of uniting the dancers as one "body," one musical instrument (referred to by DJs and dancers alike as "the crowd" or "the floor"). The dancing body, as musical instrument in both individual and collective appearance, is a defining aspect of UDM performance; this points to musical as well as social implications.

The body as musical instrument

From the perspective of the DJ booth, the dance floor is the central area of a dance venue. It provides the space for dancing as the main focus of the DJ. While his performance is in most cases a one-person affair, dancing almost always involves more than one person (although there may be moments when the dance floor is occupied by only one dancer or none at all). As the musical program is sent from the DJ booth through the sound system onto the dance floor, feedback flows from the floor to the DJ booth, mainly, but not exclusively, in the form of multiple bodily responses, that is, dancing. However, before investigating the relationship between music and dancing, let me suggest how dance, and its chief instrument, the body, may be understood.

A definition of dance

Dance can be most usefully defined as human behavior composed, from the dancer's perspective, of (1) purposeful (2) intentionally rhythmical, and (3) culturally patterned sequences of (4a) nonverbal body movements (4b) other than ordinary motor activities (4c) the motion having inherent and aesthetic value. (Aesthetic refers to notions of appropriateness and competency held by the dancer's reference groups which acts as a frame of reference for self-evaluation and attitude formation to guide the dancer's actions.) Within this conceptualization, human behavior must meet each of these four criteria in order to be classified as "dance."[4]

Sexuality and dance share the same instrument—the human body.[5]

While often concerned with cross-cultural comparisons, Judith Hanna's work, including the publications from which the above quotes are taken, has at times been criticized because of its narrow focus on the context of either non-Western traditions[6] or Western theatrical "high-culture,"[7] and because it excludes the domain of social dance as part of

Western popular culture (a cultural hybrid itself). Yet, her definitions of dance are so broad as to apply to both high art and social or vernacular dance forms. Based on these definitions, the above statements are well-suited to frame the following discussion of the body as a instrument of social and musical expression in underground club dancing.

Iain Chambers, while not a dance scholar, has commented on the body as instrument able to reflect multiple social, cultural, and musical identities and meanings. While his remarks are primarily based on his study of Western, specifically British popular music, they apply also to the environment of underground dance music in New York City.

Music can be considered an important "counterspace" in our daily lives. Its power lies in a temporary suspension of the division between the "private" and the "public," between the imagination and the routines, roles and social relations in which we regularly find ourselves locked. As such, music is not an "escape" from "reality", but an interrogative exploration of its organizing categories. Imagination and "reality" are brought together in a significant friction and exchange. And the major site of this encounter is the frequently repressed zone of the body. . . . It is the body that ultimately makes, receives and responds to music; and it is the body that connects sounds, dance, fashion and style to the subconscious anchorage of sexuality and eroticism.[8]

It is above all the body, enveloped in sound, in dance, that stands at the crossroads of pop music and leisure time. Dancing, where the explicit and implicit zones of socialized pleasures and individual desires entwine in the momentary rediscovery of the "reason of the body" (Nietzsche), is undoubtedly one of the main avenues along which pop's "sense" travels. Suspended over the predictable rhythms of the everyday, to dance often involves loaded steps, a pattern of obliquely registered tensions. These represent not only the contradictory pull between work and pleasure, but also between a commonsensical view of pleasure ("letting off steam," "a well-earned break," "enjoying yourself") and a deeper, internalized moment where a serious self-realization—sexual and social, private and public—is being pursued.[9]

When viewed in terms of the dichotomy (often assumed or taken for granted in discussions of popular music) between musical production and consumption, dancing appears as the most immediate and direct mode of consuming a music produced for dancing (named "dance floor" after all in some parts of the Western world). The act of dancing is one that takes place in a public or semipublic place,[10] on a dance floor, where the dancer voluntarily becomes, together with others, a participant in what Victor Turner has referred to as a "ritual process."[11] While there are many anthropologists who have written on dance as ritual, of interest here is one central aspect of the dance-ritual nexus: its collective aspect, which Turner refers to as "communitas."[12] In this view, dancing, as collective performance, encompasses the notion of music consumption while, at the same time, transcending it. The dancer is not merely a consumer, but rather a participant and performer in and of the musical event as well.[13] While Turner speaks of dance as ritual in general, the capacity to engender communitas through the ritual of dance is indispensable to African American expressive culture.

The body as social instrument: Dance, identity, marginality

As noted by many commentators on social dance, the pleasurable experience of the body, and the expression of that experience through dance has been, and depending on the circumstances, to some extent continues to be, perceived in opposition to, or as exception to, predominant social rules and values, particularly in U.S. American society.[14] In the context of social values and norms perceived as oppressive, the dance floor of an underground dance venue becomes, as Gotfrit states, "one location where desire and pleasure are courted and orchestrated, where the body is central, and where sexuality . . . is permitted expression."[15] She confirms Chambers' assertion that "dancing is the fundamental connection between the pleasures of sound and their social realization in the libidinal movements of bodies, styles and sensual forms. It represents a social encounter . . . where bodies are permitted to respond to physical rhythms that elsewhere would not be tolerated; [it represents] the moment where . . . a transitory step out of the everyday can be enjoyed."[16]

This type of reaction of the dancing individual to his or her perception of the general social order has consequences of subversive potential when multiplied across a packed dance floor. In an article for the *New York Times* entitled "Paradise Found, At Least for a Moment," Jon Pareles comments on dance music's "benign power to create community [via dance as ritual, as the dance floor becomes] a privileged demilitarized zone where tensions of class, generation and race are checked at the door while good times are shared."[17]

Paradise Garage, a Manhattan club that closed its doors in September 1987, was and still is regarded as having been the most influential underground dance venue in New York City. To this day many members in the underground dance scene consider it to have constituted the epitome of social dancing as a celebration of individuality and community at the same time.[18] Dance records produced after 1987 have invoked the club's name more often than any other venue in New York by either mix or song title.[19] Kevin Hedge, a member of Blaze, a New Jersey–based dance music production team, reminisced in an article about the Paradise Garage that reads like an obituary: ". . . in the Garage, we had blacks, Anglos, Jews, Spanish, gays, straights, everybody in one situation with a peaceful thing on their mind."[20] Ever since its closing, promoters and hosts at other clubs (and not just in New York, but as far as London or Tokyo) have been trying to re-capture the sound, image, and ambiance of the Paradise Garage, referring to their clientele as "family, we're all family in here."[21] On 10 May 1992, DJ Junior Vasquez celebrated the third anniversary of the club Sound Factory on West Twenty-seventh Street in Manhattan by spinning for an enthusiastic crowd of more than three thousand from Saturday midnight until Sunday 6:00 P.M. The event was billed and advertised as "Paradise Regained." Less than three years later, the closing of Sound Factory evoked a response in the local dance community similar in kind and degree as did the closing of the Paradise Garage.[22]

Having visited and danced at New York venues such as the Loft, the Choice, Paradise Garage, Club Savage, Sound Factory, Sound Factory Bar, Shelter, Afterlife, Tilt, City, Roxy, Octagon, Save The Robots, and Club Vinyl, I am in basic agreement with Hedge's and Pareles' assessments. On the dance floor of New York underground clubs, the idea of "paradise" has been repeatedly invoked or pursued in song and dance, to contrast it with that other nonparadise, the world outside, with its persistent social inequalities and violent conflicts.[23]

Inside an underground dance venue, like Paradise Garage or Sound Factory, it matters less whether the individual dancer is female or male, gay or

The last night at Paradise Garage. On Sunday, September 27, 1987, the closing of this influential dance venue marked the end of an era (the party actually did not end until Monday–nobody wanted it to). This picture was taken from Larry Levan's booth overlooking the main dance floor. *Photo © Tina Paul, 1987.*

The Paradise Garage logo, featuring the club dancers' musical instruments, the whistle and the tambourine. Once mounted over the entrance to the club, the sign is presently stored in West End Records' president Mel Cheren's house. © *West End Records.*

The building on King Street in Manhattan that used to house Paradise Garage on its second floor. This 1999 picture shows its use as a garage for vehicles of the Bell Atlantic telephone company. *Photo by the author.*

straight, as long as the collective spirit, "the vibe in the house," is one of mutual tolerance and goodwill. Repeatedly, I have heard promoters at such venues invoke this imagery when addressing their clientele over a microphone. In these clubs where the majority of patrons are often male or African American or both, dancers dance alone or with dancers of the same or the opposite sex, doing perhaps one of several versions of the hustle.[24] Nondancing men and women who may form a circle of spectators around one, two, or three dancers dancing hip-hop, freestyle, or vogue.[25] More typically, the dance movements are at the individual dancer's discretion and not prescribed (except for the occasional group routine or line dance where half the floor may spontaneously join to step in formation, doing the Bus Stop or the Electric Slide).[26] One may dance alone, anonymously, or interact with other dancers, by making eye contact, exchanging verbal comments, or copying a certain step, and taking turns with him or her in front of a crowd of spectators. Playful competition is often central in a group of male peers who take turns trying to "burn" each other with very original combinations or technically or athletically demanding moves, while the competitors look on and may give intermittent applause and/or shouts of encouragement or compliments.[27] Dancing (also deejaying) is frequently referred to as "Working (it) out," as "Work it!" or as "You better work!"—the corresponding encouragement or compliment to a particular dancer's (or DJ's) performance. This use of "work"—which might be seen as an African American inversion[28] of the central concept of the Anglo-American Protestant work ethic—is also reflected in the titles of many records.[29]

Archie Burnett, who has danced in New York underground clubs on a regular basis since 1981, considers his dancing a physical and mental workout. In his words, the DJ's efforts behind the turntables translate directly into the dancer's domain: "As you walk in, you hear and smell the sounds, which get your blood pumping and adrenaline flowing. The club itself is a mood changer. You may have had the worst day, but when you are in there for two hours, your mood will change. It's about music, energy, spirituality, all in one. But you must give yourself over to it. You have no choice because the DJ is going to make you work."[30] This type of effect on the body by the music is described in similar terms by Miezitis: "As you approach, even from a distance, you can already hear the faint beat, feel it reverberating ever so slightly in the pavement. It pulses like a heartbeat, growing with every step toward the disco entrance. . . . As you enter, electricity shoots through the air in all directions. The energy flows from the music and the lights and the crowd, from inside yourself. . . . Throughout the night, as more and more people come to a disco, the energy level builds and the interaction between the deejay and crowd intensifies."[31]

Besides the performance by a DJ and those of his dancers, there is yet another type of performance to be found inside a dance venue: that of the "showcase" disco artist or singer. A showcase takes place on a performance stage during a specific time (usually an hour or two after midnight) set aside by the venue's management or the promoter, and is usually a combination of live vocals and a playback tape. Often, the purpose of showcases is to promote a recently issued record of the performer in question (usually a single vocalist). In club terminology, the supreme compliment is to bestow on such a performer the title "diva," a compliment always given by men, most of them gay, many of them African American, to a female who is most often African American as well. Vocalists such as Donna Summer, Gloria Gaynor, Grace Jones, Rochelle Fleming, Loleatta Holloway, Martha Wash, Kim Mazelle, or Adeva are loved and adored as "divas" by their mostly male and largely gay fans. Club appearances by these "stars" of club music are best witnessed on so-called gay nights, when predominantly, but not exclusively gay audiences are known to respond to the performances of their idols more enthusiastically than straight crowds do on "straight" nights. Often during these performances, a bond between performer and audience is celebrated: both the divas, as African-American females, and their audiences, whether Caucasian, Latino, or African-American gay men, are in more than one way "others" in a society based on Western Judeo-Christian values and standards that have historically reinforced the marginalization of its minorities of Latinos, African-Americans, gays and lesbians. Nonetheless, some consider the popular image of the black diva problematic, as it may signify a gendered form of racism among white gay men, which in turn bespeaks the status of women in mainstream American society in general.[32]

If matters of privacy, etiquette, self-presentation, and sexual expression are able to be redefined via club dancing, the dance itself then is an act that has the potential to liberate the self (mind/body) from dominant modes of thinking and behavior. Dancing thus can have an educational function, impacting the way one thinks about oneself as a gendered human being, and/or about others who may belong to a different ethnic group, and/or may express a different sexual orientation. Dancing may reflect or amplify the social conditioning of one's gender, just as it may enhance the concept of one's own gender and sexuality. It can also question or even subvert these constructs ever so playfully. This option of playful subversion can facilitate the issue of self-expression in public, which is particularly relevant to those whose expressions place them at the margins of American society. Carol Cooper has linked club dancing to African American culture in which playful, yet politically charged subversion has a history so long so as to turn sexuality into what she calls "cryptosexuality":

Cryptosexuality is the art of pretending to be what you aren't because no one can come up with a satisfactory definition of what you are. It is also the art of inversion—of flipping the meanings of things inside out, the better to understand what words and music truly signify. . . . In the black community, blended gender roles are a normal manifestation of the survival instinct. Whatever you need to get out of a tight spot is what you will become. A gift of mimicry, a love of personal style, and/or the need to make an emphatic point will almost turn anyone into a screaming queen. . . . The act of subversion is fun. It is the ultimate entertainment of those who are easily bored by anything predictable and static. Playing the dozens is subversive. Voguing is subversive. And when done well, playing records in a club or on radio is subversive. The entire house movement out of Chicago brought raging polymorphous sexuality to such a height of dancefloor acceptance that explicit pornographic lyrics from icons of outrageousness like Candy J. and Karen Finley became common.[33]

Underground club dancing is thus not contingent upon fixed notions of ritualized courtship. Rather, courting through dance is one of many options. This flexibility contrasts with the concept of gender-specific courtship, according to which the Euro-American male who, through the ages that brought us the Renaissance pavane, the Viennese waltz, and the Argentinian tango, has been accorded the power to "lead" a female dance partner across a dance floor. In a patriarchal and heterosexual world, for African Americans, gays, and female dancers, then, disco and post-disco club dancing can be a political statement. Dancing can be as much about empowerment as fun. For women in particular, Gotfrit has pointed out, dancing can be a disruption and a subversion of dominant practices. Her example is the account of herself dancing with two female friends in a Toronto club named the Big Bop, in a social environment reflective of rather strongly enforced heterosexual standards: "We ruptured the Big Bop scene by assertively taking up space, and by controlling that space. We never succumbed to dancing in the dominant mode—small and repetitious gestures in a circumscribed space—but filled the space that was available. The appropriation of space exclusively for women's pleasure, control, and solidarity is radical."[34]

That may have been true for Toronto in 1991. However, close to a decade later, it is not so radical in New York clubland. Here, as in other American cities, underground dance clubs have long been closely connected to gay and/or African American subcultures, which are characteristically more tolerant of nonmainstream behavior. Still, what Gotfrit calls radical in the context of women dancing in Toronto can be extended to the context of predominantly gay underground dance clubs in New York City. Club events advertised as "specifically for women," or "women only," are still fewer in number in the context of urban nightlife where men consistently outnumber women. Three decades after the Stonewall Riots, clubgoers have become quite accustomed to designations such as "gay nights" or "straight nights." Whereas gay men in New York City were successful in carving out a subcultural niche in these clubs during the 1970s and 1980s, lesbian women have had a harder time establishing a corresponding niche for themselves where male support, let alone participation, is deemed largely undesirable or unnecessary, an idea that in itself may be as or more radical in nature than Gotfrit's concept of "disruption."

Types of gender construction and of expressions of sexuality that do not necessarily conform with mainstream values are characteristic of underground dance culture. Dancing, then, is not merely one form of musical consumption. As long as the dancer is on the floor, he or she is performing, either for him- or herself, for one or several dance partners, or for the DJ. Collectively, all dancers, through the sum total of many individual performances, offer the DJ a performance encompassing the entire dance floor. The feedback of this collective performance is the crucial instrument by which the DJ can evaluate the appeal of his program. By monitoring the dance floor, a good DJ can gauge the type of music his audience likes to dance to most—although this is hardly a constant, as the population on the floor is in constant flux as the night goes on.

Just as the technology of musical mediation is the instrument sine qua non for the production, actualization, and performance of dance music as a sonic phenomenon, the human body, through dancing, becomes the instrument sine qua non for the production, actualization, and performance of dance music as visual and physical phenomena. Unto themselves, the sonic and the kinetic spheres are incomplete parts of a form of musicking in which sound can be experienced physically, and the dancing human body acts as a musical instrument.

Music as both sound and dance, while connected to the disco concept, cannot be explained solely in its terms. Both sonically and physically, underground music and dance are closely connected to gay sensibilities found in other dance worlds as well.[35] In New York City, the development of underground dance music and the emergence of a locally distinct gay culture have long been processes of ongoing mutual influence and overlap. The role of gay sensibilities in the shaping of club music and club dancing may be easier to understand if one considers New York's discotheques and dance clubs as institutions with an integral role in the history of an emerging and progressively visible gay culture. While this cultural connection is the focus of chapter 6, the following descriptions of dance venues in New York City sorts out the differences between underground and commercial, and portrays the settings in which DJs and their audiences interact.

Clubbing in the field:
Underground dance venues in New York City

The following[36] is a club typology, based on the ways dancers conceptualize their environment (particularly the dance floor) and their dancing, as interaction with the music, or as an expression of self. At issue is how underground dancing or clubbing is understood as distinct from other contexts of social dancing, based on the understanding of underground as an environment where special rules apply concerning the body as instrument of social and musical expression and interaction.

Since the disco era of the 1970s, the nightclub industry in New York City has evolved around institutions that cover a spectrum of clubbing environment types. At one end is the type of environment where music and dancing are subordinate to other modes of socializing: eating, drinking, smoking, lounging. These environments can be restaurants, bars, or discotheques, which may feature extravagant interior decor, complete with cigarette girls offering tobacco and candy, and/or a selective door policy. Typically, music and dancing are confined to one circumscribed area, as in the basement below a dining area. The patrons of these establishments are generally perceived by underground dancers to attend for reasons other than those directly related to the music or the dance. They may not dance much, or know who the DJ is or what records he or she is playing. These types of environment are often considered "commercial" by members of the dance underground, their patrons are mocked as "tourists" (that is, not regulars) and/or "B&T"s (out-of-towners who access Manhattan by bridge or tunnel).[37]

At the other end of the spectrum of New York nightlife entertainment is the underground venue. Here, the music and the dance are considered central. Generally, the dance floor is the largest area within the premises, sometimes the only area that patrons can occupy apart from the DJ booth and the restrooms. Depending on the presence of a liquor license, alcohol may be served. Often, the absence of alcohol is stressed by the promoters or the management as part of an alternative environment to the commercial venues. Food, if provided, comes at no additional charge beyond the entry fee, and is available at a self-serve buffet (chips and/or fruit), or cooked in large quantities and served once, usually late during the night in a decidedly informal picnic-type atmosphere (say, chicken and rice on paper plates, eaten with plastic forks and spoons, in standing position unless chairs and/ or tables are available). Socializing, while important, does not diminish the dancing in terms of number of participants and time devoted to it. The patrons tend to be familiar with the DJ and his music; indeed, he (or she) is

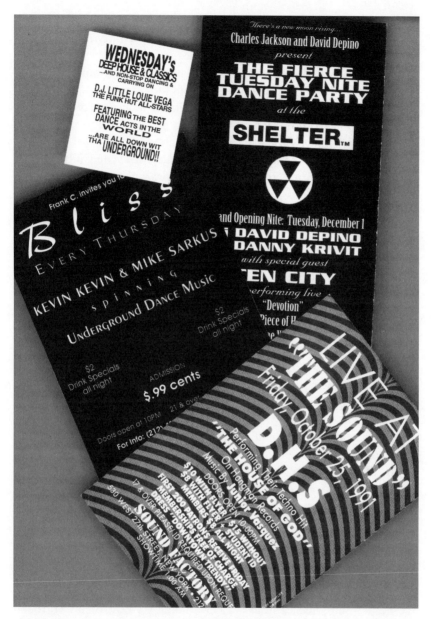

"You coming out tonight?" Flyers like these, distributed through record stores and on street corners, announce the weekly and monthly offerings of dance music around the city, advertising DJs, artist showcases, and new releases alike. Frequently, they function as reduced-admission tickets as well. *Photo by the author.*

often the main reason for their attendance. Dancers give shouts of joyful recognition of certain songs and may sing along with the lyrics. In contrast to many commercial venues, the decor at underground venues is often sparse or improvised with economical means such as balloons and hand-made designs of colored paper hanging from the ceiling and walls. A large percentage of the patrons of underground dance venues are regulars who, over time, come to know each other well enough to form a social cohesion referred to as "family," "friends," or "running buddies."

Within this range of nightlife establishments, each venue, if it manages to make a name for itself in the first place, comes with a certain identity or image cultivated by its operators. This identity is a totality formed by the elements of name, location, size, type of music, type of clientele, type of establishment (bar, restaurant, club, alcohol-free, and so forth), and admission policy (pricey, racist, "come-as-you-are").

Open from 1976 to 1987, Paradise Garage may very well have been the most influential nightclub worldwide, especially in its heyday during the early 1980s. It was a dance mecca to a group of loyal regulars, most of them gay and African American, who came every Saturday to pay homage to Larry Levan, the resident DJ, regarded as one of the most influential figures in underground dance music. Levan's eclectic style as DJ and, later, re-mixer, influenced a generation of younger DJs (earning him the title "father"[38]), and Richard Long's sound system has found no equal, even though it was duplicated at Zanzibar in Newark, New Jersey, and later installed in London's Ministry of Sound. Fortunately, in contrast to many other important underground venues, the impact of Paradise Garage has been described in considerable detail.[39]

The Shelter on Hubert Street in the Tribeca section of Manhattan became the regular spot for many underground clubheads after the closing of Paradise Garage. It had a layout of similar dimensions, a similarly designed sound system, and featured DJs who programmed in the tradition of Levan: soulful house music with many classics added after 4:00 or 5:00 A.M. Resident DJ Timmy Regisford regularly "worked" his crowd on Sunday mornings into a sea of screaming, sweating bodies. The Shelter closed in 1993 after almost four years of operation. In an attempt to offer the "Garage heads" and "Shelter heads" a new "home," a host of underground dance parties then emerged, such as House Nation, The Source, Melting Pot and Afterlife, although with limited success.[40] Most of these closed again in the mid-1990s during a period when, influenced by Mayor Guiliani's "quality-of-life" campaign, many city agencies sought to limit nightclubs, or at least to subject them to a higher level of scrutiny. Two newer parties, Body & Soul, a Sunday afternoon/evening dance at Club

Vinyl (formerly Shelter), featuring three DJs simultaneously, and Legends, at Life on Bleeker Street, have managed to survive since 1996 and 1997, respectively, due in part to the promotional skills of John Davis who handles both, and to the support of former Garage and Shelter patrons. Timmy Regisford's Shelter party, disguised as Temple for a while, reopened under its old name on Saturday nights in 1998 at the old address on Hubert Street in Tribeca.

Jackie 60 is the name of a party, not of a location. Held every Tuesday for ten years at a small bar on West Fourteenth Street named "The Bar" (where other floating underground parties such as "Clit-Club" and "Meat" have been held on Saturdays and Fridays, respectively), it is a party for mainly Manhattanites with an artistic knack for camp and out-of-the-ordinary performance art. Besides the music by DJ Johnny Dynell, Jackie 60 featured so-called theme parties including transvestite fashion shows, body-painting contests, and photo and art exhibitions. The premises consist of three rooms, two of which have a bar, the third being a basement furnished as a lounge for socializing. The clientele, while ethnically mixed, includes many white gay males who sometimes attend in costume or drag. Because Dynell and his partner, drag performer Chi Chi Valenti, bought the premises in 1997, Jackie 60 survived many other underground dance parties. The Bar, renamed Mother since the purchase, continued to host parties in 1999, but Jackie 60 events will be discontinued at the end of the millennium.

In the mid-1990s, Sound Factory on West Twenty-seventh Street and Sound Factory Bar on West Twenty-first Street had the same management, but were clubs with different histories and concepts. Sound Factory, conceptually and technologically modeled after Paradise Garage, is best described in the terms of a regular patron. It "first opened its doors to a mainly black crowd in 1989. . . . The club also gained notoriety as the battle ground for vogue houses like the Xtravaganzas, who were buzzing on the double-hype of [the films] *Paris Is Burning* and *Truth Or Dare*. By the time of its third anniversary, more and more white queens were crashing the space. . . . Those who didn't like what Sound Factory was becoming fled to Shelter, then to the similarly named, but unrelated Sound Factory Bar. Those who stuck around . . . did so because they got off on what Junior [Vasquez] was doing, pulling the Factory out of its identity crisis and turning it into the 'world-famous' House of Vasquez."[41] The club, known for its "nonalcoholic" policy, never got the liquor license required for any nightclub to stay open legally past 4:00 A.M. After six years of intermittent hassles by city authorities, the owners abruptly closed the venue. Co-owner Richard Grant explained: "Contrary to rumor, we did not lose our cabaret license. But we knew there was a danger, so we decided to close."[42] The club was subsequently reopened as Twilo, again with resident DJ Junior Vasquez, while Sound Factory moved to West Forty-sixth Street and became a venue for B&Ts.

Whereas Sound Factory was open only on weekends, Sound Factory Bar, a smaller venue that was converted from a gay videotheque, was open up to seven nights a week between 1992 and 1997. Featuring three bars, its profits from liquor sales were as important as the DJs who spun on the main dance floor once a week: during 1995, Louie Vega worked the main floor on Wednesdays, Lord G on Thursdays, Frankie Knuckles on Fridays, and David DePino on Saturdays. In the basement, called the Funk Hut for its more intimate atmosphere, DJs such as David Camacho, Kim Lightfoot, André Collins or Danny Krivit presented a musical program that often contrasted with the uptempo style upstairs due to a stronger emphasis downstairs on classic disco, funk, or reggae. It closed and reopened in 1997 as Cheetah, hosting the first openly gay hip-hop party in the city under the name Phab. In 1999, DJ Nicky Siano reopened the venue, after some renovation, as 12 West, resurrecting the name of a gay discotheque, which was originally located on West Street in Greenwich Village.

The Loft, on temporary hiatus after its fourth reincarnation in the East Village, is scheduled to reopen to celebrate its thirtieth anniversary in 2000. As such, it is "New York's longest-running underground party . . . , a private party in David Mancuso's house, which just happens to have a club for a living room. No alcohol is served, but juice and plenty of food are provided gratis. David's musical mix, played on an audiophile-quality system, ranges from underground house, to classics, to new age and jazz, to records that have no genre except that of 'Loft Classics.'"[43] The Loft patrons have a reputation as one of the most devoted groups of regular dancers; some have been clubbing regularly for more than two decades. During the Paradise Garage era, "Loft babies" and "Garage heads" conceived of each other as rival collectives. This concept of rivalry was later carried on between factions of "Shelter heads" and "Factory heads."

In the tradition of long-defunct dance clubs, such as Better Days and Tracks, promoters Mike Stone and Charles Jackson have held weekly parties at the Warehouse in the South Bronx since 1997, drawing a largely African American and gay following every Saturday night. Resident DJ André Collins, who learned by observing Nicky Siano at Gallery, believes he is successful as a DJ because he "started out as a dancer. I'm still a dancer. I think in terms of a dancer when I create a vibe. I play the tunes I know would get me moving."[44] His musical program is an energetic combination of new and old house records, with an occasional disco classic thrown in for good measure.

As a highly dynamic and ever-changing environment, New York City's dance club scene is periodically presented in journalistic overviews that appear in the local commercial press. Typically, the authors lump together all types of venues, old and new, underground and commercial, floating and those that are synonymous with or attached to a restaurant or bar.[45] The resulting spectrum is varied, and can be best described in terms of a range of environments where, on one end, the music—as it applies to dancing—is the central aspect and factors such as the qualities of the sound system, the character of the crowd, and the musical style of the DJ are crucial. On the other end, the music is only part of a scene in which glamour, attitude, fashion, style, drugs, alcohol, and the desire to see or be seen shape the dynamics of the evening and the location. Correspondingly, underground and commercial venues are located on opposite ends of this spectrum. Limelight is a good example of the latter type.

Located on Sixth Avenue at Twentieth Street, Limelight is one of the most long-lived discotheques in the city. A former church, it is owned and managed by club mogul Peter Gatien, whose organization includes other large commercial venues in Manhattan such as Tunnel and the now-demolished Palladium. Used by various promoters who bring in different crowds and DJs on different nights, Limelight is not cheap to get in. Still, long lines at the entrance doors are common due to a selective door policy (labeled racist and/or sexist by some detractors). Conceptually, Limelight is a continuation of the large, glamorous clubs of the 1970s, such as Bonds, Studio 54, and Xenon. Musically, it is known for a host of up-and-coming DJs who used to operate the very loud, but not very clear-sounding sound system from a booth installed just below the church roof, high above the dance floor.[46] Many Limelight patrons are dressy Caucasians and Asians in their twenties, among them many B&Ts. Since the mid-1990s, Limelight has been the focus of an ongoing public relations scandal involving sex, drugs, and murder. In the process, the club has been raided and locked by New York police in connection with alleged trafficking and selling of illegal drugs on the premises, only to be reopened with promises of more security and an official "zero-tolerance policy" for drugs.

The activities circumscribed and contrasted here as underground clubbing take place in an environment defined in terms of size, geography, frequency and number of participants. Whereas the total number of discotheques in New York City was estimated to peak above the one-thousand mark at the end of the 1970s,[47] the number of underground venues has always been much lower. The idea of a dancing environment accessible only to a number of initiated aficionados who "know the deal"[48] typifies the dance underground. Accordingly, underground venues do not advertise nearly on the same scale that "commercial" discos or clubs do, nor do they attempt to attract the wandering passerby, in stark contrast to "bridge-and-tunnel" clubs that either have flashy neon-lit logos over their entrance doors, or else a eye-catching cordoned-off area watched over by outrageously clad door personnel—as was the case with the beleaguered and now re-opened Limelight or the once popular and now demolished Palladium.

Dancers at underground clubs in the post-Garage period tend to follow the example of their predecessors in terms of dancing attire and attitude. At Paradise Garage, Arlene Yu recalled: "because the body was part of the self, much of the [dancer's] clothes were revealing or approximated clothing worn in the gym where many [patrons] went to work out, to work on themselves. . . . I saw here a belief in an inner, unique self, that needed to be expressed. [Paradise Garage][49] was the only place I could be myself. The inner self was worn as a badge of pride, not 'like when I have to go to work all suited up and uncomfortable with this tie strangling me.'"[50] Dancing at Paradise Garage was an experience that stood in stark contrast with the outside world. Yu's comments concerning the Paradise Garage environment apply to the city's dance underground in general: "The unique thing about the [club] was . . . its rules . . . were experienced in relation to those of an outside, straight world."[51]

Throughout my fieldwork period, the majority of my contacts—both in the dance music industry and the underground scene—perceived New York City nightlife as progressively less dynamic, especially compared to fifteen, ten, or even five years earlier.[52] This impression is corroborated by the fact that, historically speaking, there are fewer underground clubs in operation, and fewer people frequenting these remaining venues. Those who still frequent constitute a group of clubheads and hardcore dancers who avoid what they refer to as the "trendy" and "commercial" venues where "tourists, posers and B&Ts" congregate. This core group with which most of my informants identify, distinguishes itself from a generation of so-called new schoolers. These teenagers of the 1980s have grown in size so as almost to equal the older group, the "old school" of dancers in the dance clubs of New York City. Many in this new generation, however, have not made dance music their main focus. The distinction between trendy and underground applies also to the category of after-hours venues that operate, or continue to operate, after 4:00 A.M., often without licenses for assembly or alcohol as required by law. "Two types of after-hours spot have always coexisted on the New York scene, dance-oriented juice bars, where drugs are clearly in evidence, but not the whole point, and the smaller joints, where people *sit around* drinking vodka and snorting coke and talking drug babble to each other."[53]

Regarding the dance-oriented clubbers, the distinction between "old school" and "new school" is usually applied only by the members of the older segment, who view the gradual displacement of one "generation" by another with some regret. Instead of a gradual "passing of the torch"[54] from one generation of dancers to the next, the perceived difference in social sensibility between the old and the new school is evident in their attitudes, made visible in different styles of language, dress, and dancing: communal dancing involving everybody on the floor is characteristic of the older generation; individualistic dancing with circles of nondancing spectators is a common trait among new schoolers. Whereas explanations for this difference range widely, one links the circle phenomenon to the impact of Music Television (MTV) which, since the mid-1980s, has disseminated hip-hop dance styles as the visual accompaniment to video clips by nationally marketed hip-hop acts. The new-school style of demeanor, dress, and dancing is indeed very similar to that expressed in these videos. This implies a greater emphasis on visual media, at the expense of audio media (which in turn is the more influential medium for the old school).

In New York City, dancing in the underground goes beyond the translation of auditory signals into bodily movement. It is the manifestation of the possibility, the option, or the attempt to step outside the restrictions, conventions, and norms of the world beyond the doors of the dance venue. The intensity of audio and visual signals—music played at high volume with a strong exaggeration of the extremes of the audio spectrum (high and low frequencies), combined with the effects of remote-control light beams and laser beams, fog machines and stroboscopes—is apt, indeed designed, to lead to other-than-everyday sensations on the part of the dancer. This feeling of otherworldliness, particularly when combined with the heightened physical energy of dancing, is essential to the "disco experience."

This feeling may also explain why dance venues have been consistently associated with the consumption of mind-altering substances.[55] Dancing in this environment may be a private experience ("'Oh shit, that's my record! Gotta go [and dance]!'"),[56] but more typically is done in interaction with others, a partner, a group of friends, or as a stranger among many other strangers with whom the dance space is shared. This configuration gives the participants the permission to redefine the social rules of the everyday world. Dancing is first of all a physical act; hence, one's own dancing body interacting with the music is the central source of sensation. However, it is also a social act, with potentially far-reaching consequences. On the dance floor, the dancing body engages in a private language in a public sphere. Dancing thus becomes a performance in which the private and public spheres are redefined in ritual form. Dancing, or "working (it) out." translates into a ritual in which the physical aspect of self, the body, is the instrument for renewing the spiritual or mental aspect of self, that is, the nonphysical aspects of identity.[57]

Interactive performance: The musical process and cultural context of underground dance music

So far, I have discussed deejaying and dancing as autonomous, yet interdependent expressive activities, and as such, characteristic traits of UDM in New York. Accordingly, spinning is the DJs domain, and involves the creative use of his equipment—records, turntables, mixer, and a sound system. Working it out is determined by each individual dancer's efforts. He or she determines the degree to which the dance will interact not only with the music, but also with the dancing of others on the same floor. While the variables of space, lighting, musical program, and other factors contributing to the "vibe" may be reflected, the dance itself is an autonomous individual creation (freestyle) and its author is at liberty to determine the degree to which elements of certain dance styles (for example, hustle, vogue, breakdancing) may be incorporated. Yet spinning and dancing are closely interdependent. A good DJ will animate his dancers to react to his music; in turn, ferocious and/or creative dancing will prompt a DJ to program and mix his music correspondingly.

At issue then is the nature of the link between music and dance in the practice of the New York underground. Of interest are the conditions that allow for the close interaction between the type of musicking particular to the DJ booth and that to the dance floor, and how this interaction is shaped and structured. The discussion which follows is based on the observation that, in practice, the interaction happens almost instantaneously. The simultaneity of two processes marked both by a high degree of creative autonomy requires a regulatory mechanism of synchronization. The synchronization can be said to have two aspects: a musical synchronizer (rhythm) and a cultural synchronizer (the underground) work together to allow for a direct and seemingly instantaneous line of communication. The synchronization of mediated music and dancing as collective performance through rhythm will be the subject of the following chapter, whereas the underground as cultural catalyst will be the topic of chapter 6.

Conclusion: Keep on dancing

The concept of collective performance is central to a discussion of underground dancing. While the idea of performance applies equally to the

DJ and the dancer, it is the multiplication, across a densely populated dance floor, of each individual dancer's physical response that gives club dancing its collective character as it transforms sound into movement in a generally unstructured and playful fashion. At clubs like Paradise Garage, playing with and playing the body as musical instrument fuse.[58]

Potential bearer of multiple meanings in social, political, and sexual terms, the dancing body turns into a most expressive as well as versatile instrument. As the carrier of a sexual identity, the dancing body has been particularly relevant to those lesbians and gays whose expressions of sexuality have been controversial, if not taboo, in Western society. In the aftermath of the sociopolitical reconfigurations in the U.S. during the 1960s, the discotheque became one of the central institutions of an gay culture emerging from invisibility, attracting other marginal segments of society (African Americans, Latinos) as well. Many of New York City's influential DJs, such as Francis Grasso, Nicky Siano, Larry Levan, Frankie Knuckles and Junior Vasquez, got their start in gay discotheques, and built their reputation on a largely gay following. Levan's reign at Paradise Garage, as well as Knuckles' rise to "Godfather of House" at the Warehouse in Chicago, or Junior Vasquez's long-term association with Sound Factory/Twilo cannot be explained without considering the consistent support these (and other) influential DJs had and have in gay communities and beyond.[59]

As these communities—and by extension, American society at large—were adversely affected in the 1980s by the advent of AIDS, crack cocaine, and economic difficulties, urban nightlife underwent a series of changes. As a new generation of dancers reached clubbing age, it encountered a scenario that significantly differed from the one experienced by their elder peers. Because dance music production in the late 1980s became almost completely dominated by MIDI technology, one result was a more homogeneous sound from record to record. Simultaneously, a younger generation of DJs seemed less concerned with "teaching, leading, working" or "peaking" their floors, and tended to be less experimental, which only contributes to the musical homogeneity. DJ Troy Parrish relates this phenomenon to the increasing number of people who call themselves DJs. "There are so many more DJs now. Just because they buy a couple of records or CDs, they think they are a DJ. They're not. There's more than that to being a DJ. These days, they are all afraid to put themselves out there and teach their floors, which they are supposed to do; instead, they stick to one musical formula, one musical style"[60]

Still, or perhaps in response to more predictable programming on the part of DJs, dance music styles diversified. Whereas a DJ such as Levan was known for his eclecticism, later club DJs became classified according to musical category. For example, hip-hop or reggae DJs do not generally work at house clubs, house DJs infrequently play reggae, and techno DJs do not attract many house dancers. In New York, this trend has persisted throughout the 1990s.

Beginning in the mid-1980s, the diversity of dance music types ranging from disco to Chicago house to New York electro, from Bronx-based hip-hop and its cousins in Washington, D.C. (go-go) and in Florida (Miami bass) to Latin freestyle, from eurodisco to hi-NRG to Detroit techno, represented not only a diversification of musical styles, but also a fragmentation of dance music practitioners, industries, and audiences.[61] While it is sometimes seen as contrasting with the uniformity of late 1970s' disco, this perspective does not take into account that disco, along with funk and reggae, was generally understood to be marginal to begin with.[62] In the 1980s, the division of popular music into clusters of "styles"[63] or "genres"[64] was not just a reflection of the restructuring of the recording industry, but also of the divisions of a society in the grip of economic recession. In America's collective memory, disco was the exception to the rule precisely because it unexpectedly crossed over to the mainstream. Thus to many who lived through the period, disco is to popular music what Vietnam is to American politics at the end of the twentieth century—a bad memory. Significantly, house music, the electronic child of disco, has not crossed over in the United States. In Europe, however, especially in the United Kingdom, it became transformed (under the moniker acid house) into techno, hardcore, and rave music, all of which eventually became part of the popular music scene there.[65] In America, house has remained largely underground, shunned by the media, and continues to be associated with an urban, primarily non-Caucasian and/or gay core following.

FIVE

Underground Dancing
Autonomy and Interdependence in Music and Dance

"Ride the Rhythm."
— *On The House,* featuring Marshall Jefferson, Trax Records, 1986

Interactive performance: Synchronicity beyond simultaneity

Interactive performance is an analytic concept applicable to the mutual dependency of two forms of musicking in the context of UDM: deejaying and dancing. It implies that without the presence of dancing, spinning records loses its meaning and vice versa. In addition, the relationship is continually negotiated according to the particular ideas, attitudes, motivations, and goals of those involved. In contrast to other environments where either the music or the dance are structurally fixed or largely predetermined (by a program, a "set" of songs, or learned dance steps), there is a great deal of autonomy on both the part of the underground DJ and of the underground dancer with regard to the respective mode of performance. The performance of UDM thus provides a unique context for the study of the autonomy and interdependence of the participants. A fixed dimension (music encoded in the grooves of 12-inch vinyl recordings) in simultaneous combination with an unpredictable, spontaneous dimension (the DJ's musical program and art of spinning) affect, on an individual as well as collective level, the dancer's response to the music. Conversely, the response from the dance floor, in the form of the sum of individual responses is continually evaluated by a DJ who, for hours on end, is involved in structuring his or her musical program. Thus, the uniqueness of underground dance music lies not only in a particular combination of musical mediation and musical immediacy, but also in the positioning of mediated music at the heart of a complex whole in which music and dance, performance and reception, production and consumption are inextricably intertwined, and simultaneously, and often spontaneously, enacted.

Youngerman is one of many dance researchers who cites the relationship between music and dance as an obvious concern of dance research. She extends Blacking's model of the music-society homology to encompass dance as well.[1] I propose both music and dance are not only the result of, or homologous to, human organization, but that they are manifestations of the interactive relationship Blacking and Youngerman refer to. And, because they are types of human interaction that in turn are interdependent, they need to be treated, explored, and understood as such.

In an underground club, the simultaneity of music and dance provides a premise for their interdependence. Simultaneity does not, however, explain how this interdependence is enacted, negotiated and maintained. The basis of the relationship of sound and movement in underground dance clubs is what I call a principle of synchronicity. Synchronicity is a type of simultaneity that goes beyond the mere circumstance of co-temporal occurrence. Synchronicity implies that a dynamic relationship between music and dancing cannot be explained solely by their simultaneous occurrence. Rather, synchronicity goes beyond simultaneity by implying a relationship regulated by a synchronizing element. In the context of UDM, this synchronizing element appears to be musical rhythm, the element common to both music as sound and dancing as movement. Rhythm, above other variables, operates at the level of interactive performance of music and dance in a give-and-take fashion. It functions as a synchronizer, regulating the amounts of energy contained and communicated through both the DJ's music and the dancer's dancing.

Underground clubbers use the term *vibe* to refer to this level of energy as it appears to them, either through the music as the result of the DJ spinning, or through the varied yet synchronized moving bodies on the dance floor. This vibe is shaped by variables such as the size of the venue, the lighting, the patrons, the time of night, the dress code—in addition to the volume, tempo, and style of the music, which may or may not change from record to record, from minute to minute, or from hour to hour. Despite its elusive nature, the vibe is central to the interactive performance of DJ and dancers. And both the musical program and the dancing are key to the vibe. Of particular interest in this context is the preeminent role of rhythm as a synchronizing force, facilitating the process in which a vibe is created, shaped, changed, and maintained.

Vibe: the booth–floor interaction

On that floor—even if you don't dance—I want you to feel what I am feeling. You can't see it. You can't hold it. But you can feel it.

It's not the movement, but the music. What gets me are the drums and bass lines. . . . What propels me are the syncopations between the drums and the bass. . . . When it's good, and I hear it, it literally makes me get butterflies in my stomach. To get loose you need to be exposed to it a lot. I try to make my body the music, become one with the song.[2]

A true clubhead like Archie is obsessed with dancing—he calls it an addiction. Clubbing two to seven nights a week, putting in a minimum of 15 hours a week dancing, dancers like him are what make a club worth going to. Even a small group of these devoted movers can heat up a floor, generating a core of action that pulls people into the beat.[3]

These statements may be understood as attempts to explain the source of energy and excitement that, to a participant, can make a visit to a dance club the kind of transforming experience many have struggled to capture in writing. Echoing the sentiments of many club regulars who, in the past and present, frequent New York's underground clubs such as Paradise Garage, the Loft, the Shelter/Club Vinyl, or Sound Factory, they attempt to verbalize something that is easier conveyed through music and dance than in language. It is easier to observe the way sound can translate into physical motion and become expressive dancing, and the way this type of expressive physicality can affect other participants, both others dancers and the DJ who, through his spinning, directs this flow of energy in the first place.

In an underground dance club, music and dance not only complement each other, they affect each other. Music, as structured in the DJ booth, travels to the dance floor as a sonic phenomenon. The dance, manifest as a phenomenon more physical than sonic, is in turn structured by each individual dancer. Collectively, all dancing on the floor creates a collective energy that feeds back to the DJ booth, both on a visual as well as nonvisual level. This loop of nonverbal interaction between DJ and dancers, this type of energy exchange, is what helps shape a vibe. The vibe coming from the DJ booth may propel a dancer onto the dance floor, or may cause him or her to change the energy level of the dance. Conversely, the vibe from the dance floor may determine the programming in the DJ booth, and the way a particular record is "worked." Vibe thus describes a collective energy that can be experienced on an individual basis as well. Vibe may in fact be that form of energy that collapses the boundaries between individual and collective musical experience, an energy made possible when the music transcends the acoustic realm and becomes physical. I shall look at this aspect more closely when I discuss the dynamic properties of UDM performance. Finally, vibe carries a culture-specific meaning as a term of African American Vernacular English. Referring to both energy and atmosphere, vibe is meaningful especially for culture bearers of the African American tradition and those who have learned its idiom.[4] The cultural underpinnings of UDM, however, will be examined more thoroughly in the next chapter.

The regulation and channeling of energy between booth and floor is facilitated through the prioritization of rhythm as the central musical element of UDM. Above other musical aspects, such as timbre, tempo, amplitude, and vocal expressiveness, rhythm acts as an overriding principle on both the sonic and the physical level. By sharing a prioritization of rhythm, music and dance are compatible dimensions of underground clubbing, with the potential and intention to fuse into one experience. How is that different from many other environments of social dancing? Couldn't the claim be made that rhythm (or pulse) tends to synchronize music and dance in many other settings as well? How is the role of rhythm in the performance of UDM essentially different from its role in other dance environments?

An essential performance trait of UDM is the simultaneous presence of interdependency and autonomy on both the sonic and physical levels. The DJ bears the sole responsibility for the music, including his choice of records, his style of mixing, how long a particular record will play or when to change volume, timbre, tempo, or style. In most situations, the DJ is confined to working inside the DJ booth for hours on end. By contrast, not only is each dancer free to stay on or away from the floor as long as he pleases, his dance style and intensity are also largely a matter of personal discretion. How then does rhythm in music and dance regulate the two levels of musicking, helping to shape the vibe that makes each night, each DJ, each dance venue, each crowd of dancers unique and different from all others?

Rhythm as primary link between sound and motion

To observe a club DJ working in his booth, and to observe as well the adjacent dance floor where the dancers work out is to witness two activities very different in character (even in situations where the DJ is moving his body to the music as well), yet closely linked aspects of one and the same musical experience. It seems reasonable then to look at shared or overlapping characteristics in order to examine the relationship of the physical and sonic levels of UDM.

The most obvious common feature is the musical pulse. The pulse rate, which determines the tempo of the music, is not only one of the most noticeable features in UDM; it also underlies all dance movements. In DJ terminology, the term for tempo or pulse is *bpm* (beats per minute), and its increase or decrease, in minute or very apparent increments are entirely the DJ's responsibility. Bpm are most commonly used to pace or shape the flow of a night of UDM. The majority of UDM repertoire is produced and played in the realm of 115 to 130 bpm, with 120 to 125 bpm often used to describe the character of most club or house music. This tempo is in almost all cases structured in $\frac{4}{4}$ meter, as well as larger musical phrases which are simple divisions or, more often, multiples of four measures: 2, 4, 8, 16, 24, 32 etc.

MACRORHYTHM: REPERTOIRE, SETS, AND PACING

The relative predictability of tempo, meter, and phrase structure, once established, counterbalances the (again relative) lack of predictability of the actual repertoire. Some DJs are known to emphasize a particular subcategory of UDM during certain hours of the night (say, new records between midnight and 2:00 A.M., or classics at 5:00 or 6:00 A.M., or a preponderance of tracks as opposed to vocals).

When they first get there, they'll dance to anything 'cause they just want to start dancing. But if you put something on in the middle of the night and they don't know it, you'll get people that leave [the floor]. Or hopefully they may have heard it once or twice if they've come real early, 'cause that's when I experiment with new things, 'cause I want to personally hear how they sound large. If I start at nine [o'clock], I'm going to start playing everything brand new I just got in the last week or so, or that night even—new. Like right now I'm playing about ten different things on tape that aren't out yet—won't be out for a while. 'Cause at my house, no matter how I listen, or in a record store—when you play it on a big sound system, things change. In a club, a song comes to life. You hear it in the store, you say that sounds great. You get it into a club, it's like, oh my God![5]

David DePino, quoted above, learned to deejay while working security at the Paradise Garage, under the tutelage of Larry Levan. Levan in turn learned about mixing from DJs who worked during the peak of the disco era, especially David Mancuso and Nicky Siano,[6] who used the concept of "sets." During an interview with Steven Harvey, Levan discusses this approach, which was possibly adopted from the era when live dance bands played sets or songs of contrasting musical moods to their audiences.

HARVEY: When I first heard you play, I noticed you would sometimes leave
  spaces in between [records] or create introductions for them.
LEVAN: That's from Nicky Siano. He believed in sets. Out of all the records you

have, maybe five or six make sense together. There is actually a message in the dance, the way you feel, the muscles you use, but only certain records have that. Say I was playing songs about music—"I Love Music" by the O'Jays, "Music" by Al Hudson, and the next record is "Weekend." That's about getting laid, a whole other thing. If I was dancing and truly into the words and the feeling and it came on it might be a good record but it makes no sense because it doesn't have anything to do with others. So, a slight pause, a sound effect, something else to let you know it's a new paragraph rather than one continuous sentence. . . . Nicky Siano, David Mancuso, Steve D'Aquisto and Michael Capello, David Rodriguez from The Ginza—this is the school of DJs that I come from. David Mancuso was always very influential with his music and the mixes. . . . When I listen to DJs today [1983], they don't mean anything to me. Technically some of them are excellent—emotionally they can't do a thing for me. I used to watch people cry in The Loft [Mancuso's dance venue] for a slow song because it was so pretty. The way people party now, . . . everything has got to be wild and crazy and electronic.[7]

Whereas Mancuso, who kept his Loft open well into the 1990s despite several address changes, is not currently playing records for Loft members, Siano returned to New York in 1998 after a lengthy absence to resume deejaying, using the same approach when spinning.

No matter how familiar a DJ's taste or repertoire are to his dancers, the tempo and musical structures are areas so established as to have become matters of convention, tradition, and comfort. By contrast, the element of surprise is ever present with regard to what record will actually be played next. The tension and balance between expectation and surprise is part of what binds together a DJ and his crowd. This tension and balance is what every DJ strives to manage and maintain during the evening. Crucial in this context is the overall time allotted to the DJ. This can vary from "guest spots" which can be as short as one or two hours, to marathon shifts that can last in excess of twelve hours. In New York, short guest spots are relatively rare. However when on tour abroad—especially in European venues, which close much earlier than those in New York City—underground DJs have had to deal with short performance time frames. Frankie Knuckles comments on these situations, in which he sees himself having to start and finish his musical program "at 100%. There is just no time to build and pace. They expect me to come in and give it my all right from the start" (personal communication, January 1995).

Being able to gradually pace a dancing crowd is directly related to overall performance time. Most underground DJs (see statements by DePino and Vasquez in chapter 3) understand the large-scale flow or structure of deejaying during the course of a night as pacing. Pacing is a type of macrorhythm, even though that term is not used. To a DJ, the relationship between music and time is always critical, both on a small and large scale. To a dancer, questions of time are equally important, both during the dance as instantaneous translation of sound into motion, or else as exhaustive and exhausting workout, structured by a balance of stretches of time given to exertion versus relaxation. Therefore, within the confines of performance time and the conventions of tempo and musical structure, both underground DJs and dancers negotiate their respective performances by prioritizing rhythm on both macro- and microtime levels. With regard to the latter, the DJ has an arsenal of musical and technological options that fall into two main categories: dynamics and timbre.

RHYTHM AND DYNAMICS

UDM is played at high volume levels. For most of my visits to dance venues, I have used ear protection, and if I forget my custom-fit set of plastic plugs, I do as many other dancers who use shredded and balled-up parts of a paper napkin. In this fashion I have been largely able to avoid the unpleasant ringing in the ear resulting from extended exposure to high frequencies played at high volume. What is the point of playing at a high volume? David DePino argues that "a song comes to life" only in this way. At underground dance venues, the dynamic level of the music establishes the latter's absolute priority over other acoustic phenomena: conversation, handclapping, footstomping, yelling, whistling. All these are overshadowed by the volume of the music. The authority of the DJ is thus confirmed acoustically. "It's amazing, how loud music raises the senses. It makes the heartbeat go faster, it allows you to go emotionally into the music. You know, the kids like their music loud" says Marshall Swiney, a long-term club dancer (personal communication, January 1995).

In New York City, the work of audio engineer Richard Long seems to have set a standard in terms of sound reinforcement for dance venues. Long was the sound engineer for club owner Michael Brody at Paradise Garage. Designing its sound system in close collaboration with DJ Larry Levan, he helped to establish a sound environment that made him and Levan local legends in their lifetime. Knuckles commented on their collaboration:

This was right around the time that the movie *Earthquake* was coming out. And he [Richard] designed the Earthquake bass speakers. For the [release of the] film *Earthquake*, . . . he had this big party and he had me play at that party and he was testing the speakers at that party. And I remember the first time he tried testing them out, the ceiling collapsed in his apartment from the vibration. So he had to go back and redo the whole thing and when he finally got it right, then he had this party, with these speakers backed up against the wall . . . and I remember Larry came in and said "You should probably lay those down," because they were stacked all the way up to the ceiling. . . . And so Richard was like "No, why should I want to lay them down?" So Larry looked at me and said: "Well, correct me if I'm wrong, but didn't you say that bass should be felt and not heard?" Which is what he always taught us: "Bass should be felt and not heard." So he said yeah, and so Larry goes

"Don't you think everybody would feel better if they [the speakers] were laying down on their sides because the bass would hit everybody in their ass. And everybody would feel it in their body as opposed in their head, or hearing it in their head." And then Richard stopped for a minute and then he had the whole crew pull these speakers down and lay them down.[8]

Miezitis describes the effect of dance music with its low frequencies traveling far beyond the dance floor, by comparing the beat of the music to the human heartbeat.[9] The analogy of the musical pulse to a human heartbeat is indeed shared by many, especially dancers. Brahms LaFortune, an underground dance veteran, believes that "certain bass tones are created so you don't hear, you feel them. It is intentional—the equivalent of your heart on the outside of your body."[10]

Yu describes the effect the volume of sound in the Paradise Garage had on her: "The music was so loud, louder than anything I had ever heard. I felt the bass register of sound reverberating through my chest, had felt it since I began walking up the entrance ramp. I wanted to dance."[11] "The Garage sound system was designed as one of the loudest disco systems, while remaining also one of the clearest and described as the best. I would leave every week with nary a headache, though a lesser level (of especially the bass) would be—and was—extremely irritating and painful at other nightclubs."[12] After Long's death, engineer Steve Dash transferred the tradition established at the Garage to Sound Factory (which he co-owned). "We decided to build what we thought would be a unique system. The Paradise Garage had been closed for three or four years prior to when we decided to open, and nobody in the city decided to follow in their footsteps which really surprised us."[13] In a article on the Sound Factory sound system published in 1994, the author compares Dash's vision with the results:

Sound Factory is nationally renowned as having one of the clearest and most powerful audio systems. . . . The sound which is extremely intelligible, is entirely concentrated on the 60×60 dance floor, and there is a decibel drop as you walk off. Says Dash: "We have four speaker stacks in each corner, and on the side of the floor, blowing in, are two hanging side-fill custom-made boxes. There are no other speakers anywhere else. They're set back and pointed toward the floor, and are designed to fill the corners." Delay lines ensure that the audio hits . . . the floor at the same point in time.[14]

The above terminology of audio "blowing in," "hitting," "reverberating in my chest," or "feeling the bass" reflect the high volume level of UDM when performed. The music is not to be experienced merely sonically, but physically as well. To this end, to the extent possible, the acoustic properties of the music are pushed to approach the physical character of the dance. In this sense, the physicality of musical rhythm and/or volume is reflected in numerous song titles.[15]

However, volume and low frequencies alone are not the sole characteristics of the sound of UDM. A DJ can be seen manipulating the speed controls on his turntables or the volume controls on his mixer as much as the controls that make for the above-mentioned clarity and intelligibility of the music. These controls govern the frequency spectrum of human audio sensitivity, and are usually referred to as "EQ" (for equalizer) or crossover. Frequency control at the volume levels used in dance club environments is crucial to customer satisfaction. Al Fierstein, president of a New York sound consulting and manufacturing firm, speaks of volume as sound pressure, and so relates volume and frequency in reference to disco music.

The sound pressure levels that peak in the disco environment should generally be low frequencies, because they are less damaging to the ear than mid or high frequencies. . . . In order for a disco to be exciting, it is important for the overall level of the music to be loud. However, the highs that are present should be at a lower volume level than the lows. The reason that the low frequencies should be boosted is that they cause pressure on the total body while the mid and high frequencies only create pressure on the ears. Loudness in the upper ranges does not cause people to dance but rather to run in the opposite direction.[16]

Shannon continues by asserting, and then proving with what he calls "a statistically valid, semi-controlled experiment,"[17] that merely through an increase of volume, when properly equalized, the number of dancing patrons can be increased. The point here is not to disregard the points made earlier about the importance of programming, or to validate or invalidate Shannon's hypothesis and experiment, but to note the relationship between volume and frequency. A second important observation is the connection between low frequencies and dance stimulation. Most 12-inch recordings of dance music are mastered with more bass frequencies than the average pop or rock record. This is what dancers seem to react to, and this is what Burnett refers to in his above statement: "What gets me are the drums and bass lines. . . .What propels me are the syncopations between the drums and the bass." Frequencies of course are experienced as sound, instrument, or tone color, but their capacity to stimulate dancers is linked to a rhythmic impulse.

RHYTHM AND SOUND

Timbre is not a term used in the club scene. Sound is the preferred term, often divided in terms of frequency ranges used by the sound equipment industry. Accordingly, DJs and many dance music enthusiasts distinguish between highs, mids, and lows, and are familiar with the technology available to manipulate the spectra of audible sound: equalizers and crossovers have become part of standard DJ booth equipment, both in cheaper integrated versions, as well as stand-alone professional units costing hundreds of dollars each. A commonly used three-way crossover unit allows a DJ to decrease and increase the presence of three predetermined frequency ranges, usually labeled highs, mids and lows. Equalizers allow finer subdivisions of the frequency spectrum into bands which can be attenuated to make up for differences between individual records. Ressler makes that point, using DJ Junior Vasquez as an example:

Soundwise, his main concern is to avoid overdriving the system to the point where it will distort and hurt the dancers' ears. In addition to his seamless mixes, part of Vasquez' brilliance lies in his working the [Sound] Factory's custom crossovers and its three-way and five-way EQs. "It's like second nature to me at this point because all records aren't mastered the same . . . I have to constantly EQ and make minor adjustments after I mix a record."[18]

Other New York club DJs, including Tony Humphries, Frankie Knuckles, David DePino, Danny Tenaglia, Danny Krivit, or Louie Vega work their equipment in a similar fashion. One particularly memorable experience took place during the night of 19 January 1991, when DJ Tony Humphries, during a guest spot appearance at Sound Factory Bar, playfully exaggerated the low end by cranking the bass frequency dial on the crossover unit rhythmically in sync with the quarter-note pulse of the record he was playing.[19] The reaction from the floor came promptly in the form of gratified yells, hollers, and screams whenever he boosted the bass during the first measure of music in an eight-measure phrase, on each of the four downbeats, achieving such an exaggerated boom-boom-boom-boom effect that I saw some dancers literally trying to scale the walls. The effect reminded me of the simultaneous humor and over-the-top drama a circus band might use to accompany a trapeze act.

However dissimilar in musical background and taste, most underground DJs use dynamics and timbre controls to emphasize and enhance the rhythmic dimension unique to a particular record, so as to stimulate a more intense expressive or emotional reaction from the dancers. While there appear to be at least four different aspects to the synchronization of music and dance at an underground club, they all, in some way, pertain to, or are related to, rhythm.

On the most fundamental level, the musical tempo—made explicit through a constant pulse that is less often implied and more often very much audible, even through the walls of the dance venue—influences repertoire selection as well as setting the basic energy level for the dance floor. Counteracting the element of unpredictability and surprise concerning the selection and timbral and dynamic manipulation of repertoire, this pulse synchronizes the act of spinning with that of dancing. On a secondary level, musical considerations of dynamics and sound are controlled and manipulated by the DJ so as to heighten the rhythmic character of a given record (which, as mentioned above, in most cases is already emphasized in the production process fixed in the record's grooves).

The combined control of tempo, repertoire, dynamics, frequency distribution, as well as repertoire give the DJ control of, and responsibility for, the flow of events on the dance floor. As the technology of sound manipulation, recording, and reinforcement changed, so did the approaches to record production in the hands of DJs who had turned remixers and producers. In the following, I sketch this process, which began in the disco period and is continuing through the 1990s, using four representative 12-inch singles.

Changing modes of dance music production: A comparison of four 12-inch dance singles

To give an impression of the range of repertoire of club DJs and of changes that have occurred in the modes of production, consumption, and interaction among participants in the culture of underground dance music, I shall compare four musical examples that represent typical phases in the evolution of underground dance music since the disco period. The authors of early disco worked within the practices established by the recording industry during the 1960s. Accordingly, this tradition included multitrack technology, studio musicians and, through the influence of radio, the hegemony of the 3- to 4-minute pop song, with its typical structure including a number of verses and refrains. The introduction of the 12-inch single in 1975 made that year important for the development of dance music. The pop song format was from then on expanded, initially through the addition of longer introductions, and the insertion of long instrumental sections called "breaks." The concept of the "version" emerged, which led to the concept of the "remix."

The musical theory that served as a framework for the production of dance music on 12-inch records, each version lasting up to ten minutes or longer, came from DJ practice. During the 1970s, DJs began to construct a seamless musical program for their dancers, extending songs and sections of songs as much as possible to prolong the dancing pleasure. The transfer of this concept of extension and expansion from the DJ booth to the recording studio paved the way for the DJ making the switch from record player to mixer to remixer to artist.[20] During this transition, which gradually spanned a decade or so, the modes of producing dance music changed as well.

First Choice's "Dr. Love," released on Salsoul Records in 1977, is now considered a classic. The extended version, crafted by Shep Pettibone, lasts for more than eight minutes, and all the features that can be associated with the then popular "Philadelphia Sound" of East Coast disco are present: an easily recognizable song form that includes a modulation to distinguish verses and refrains; a lush texture achieved through the use of string and horn sections; the absence of programmed analog (and obviously digital) muical instruments, as all instruments are played by studio musicians; and the nod to gospel and soul through the use of a highly melismatic lead singer, Rochelle Fleming, set off by background vocalists, Annette Guest and Ursula Herring.

The New York City Peech Boys' "Don't Make Me Wait," released in 1982 on West End Records, is a good example of what Harvey calls "underground disco."[21] This 12-inch single features an extended version on the A-side lasting 7:14, and a dub mix on the B-side, lasting 5:52. The production credits are shared between the band's keyboardist, Michael deBenedictus, and Larry Levan. The imprint of Levan's eclectic DJ style is particularly evident in the dub mix, with its excessive use of echo, the addition of a distorted rock guitar, and the layering of several ostinati that hide the song form possibly implied by the presence of a B-section contrasting with the A-section containing the vocal refrain that gives the piece its title. A Linn drum machine has taken over the drummer's function, replacing Peech Boys drummer Steven Kendall Brown, who plays a trap set on only one of six cuts (released on the album *Life Is Something Special*), signaling the increased use of machines in dance music production in general.

Master C&J's "Face It" dates from 1987, and in its minimalism is an example of classic Chicago house. House music got its name in Chicago in the mid-1980s, at a gay club named the Warehouse where a New York DJ, Frankie Knuckles, had been offered the position of resident DJ after his friend Larry Levan had turned it down. All instruments are synthesized and programmed, and the instrumentation is typically sparse. Drum and bass ostinati are prominent, and provide a hypnotic soundscape over which male vocals—spoken, not sung—and synthesized pads of chords weave in and out. Lacking a traditional song structure, "Face It" comes in a vocal and a dub version, lasting 6:50 and 3:50, respectively.

Grampa's "She's Crazy" is a 1993 release on the now defunct independent New Jersey–based label Movin' Records. Producer Kerri Chandler pokes fun at the concept of the vocalist as artist, so prevalent in disco and pop music, by substituting the sampled voice of his grandfather who again speaks, not sings, the title phrase. This piece of dance music is farthest from the song-based concept that informs "Dr. Love" and to an extent, "Don't Make Me Wait." Instead, it is a computer-generated track, all instrumental sounds being controlled by digital processes, in this case, sequencing and sampling. The vocal sample of Chandler's grandfather is not only a mock-lead vocal, set off against an instrumental accompaniment as is the case in the First Choice example. It also becomes part of the multilevel texture, which is made up of several loops and ostinati lasting one, two and four bars each. In contrast to the earlier selections, the drum sounds are mixed very upfront, and contribute to Chandler's signature sound, which is recognized by underground dancers as "very bumpy." The 12-inch single offers DJs a choice of four mixes, all at 124 bpm, indicating a general preference for slightly faster tempos in 1990s underground dance music productions. By contrast, the previous examples ran at 115, 114, and 121 bpm, respectively.

Conclusion: Feel the vibe

As David DePino put it, UDM "comes to life" in the interactive performance relationship between DJ and dancers. This interaction is facilitated through a shared emphasis on a musical rhythm that can be distinguished as taking place both on a micro- and a macrolevel of performance. On the microlevel of rhythm, DJ and dancers interact by maintaining a balance between constant features (pulse, meter, musical structure) and variable features (dynamics, sound, and repertoire). On the macrolevel, the music may be organized in sets, or according to style or tempo or overall energy level. Combined, these considerations fall under the concept of programming. Programming is understood as an art that puts the DJ in the position of authority. The success of the ongoing interaction with the dance floor is his or her responsibility, the programming of sound and lights helping to create the vibe, which in turn determines the quality of a particular club experience.

In musical terms, rhythm joins the sonic and physical aspects of UDM performance. The energy exchange between booth and floor, the maintenance of a vibe, cannot be explained convincingly in terms of musical performance only. Rather, there is a larger context, a shared cultural dimension that enables DJ and dancers to interact in this fashion, marked by what Small, discussing the development of jazz, has called tension between freedom and order.[22] Indeed, the interdependence of a rhythm section and a soloist in a jazz ensemble is comparable to that of DJ and dancers. The rhythm section shares with the DJ a focus on pulse and structure (harmonic and/or rhythmic), providing a foundation on which the soloist can "dance." Similarly, both the jazz rhythm section and the jazz soloist are relatively autonomous in their domains, as they are expected to make their own choices in terms of timbre, pitch, volume, phrasing, and execution, in relation to the performances of each member of the ensemble.

One reason for this comparison is the common ground of jazz and UDM: the African American cultural heritage. To understand the underlying basis of UDM performance, it is necessary to connect its musical traits to the relevant cultural context. The following chapter is concerned with those two cultural environments at the margins of mainstream America in which UDM was conceived and has been developing since: black culture and gay culture.

SIX

The Underground as Cultural Context
The Marginality of Ethnic and Sexual Minorities

"Let No Man Put Asunder."
—First Choice, Gold Mind Records, 1977

In this chapter, I shall examine the cultural context of UDM. This examination is based on the premise that UDM is a cultural expression equally linked to elements of gay and black cultures, and that these cultures are both marginal to American society in general. In this context, I view music and dancing in relation to concepts of ethnic and sexual marginality, as understood, explained, and enacted by the participants in underground dance music in New York City. Because both music and dancing are actualized at a discotheque or dance club, these institutions are the primary sites of this cultural context. Inside a club, music and dance are experienced collectively as potential vehicles of identity formation and celebration; aspects of a secular, sociopolitical nature (associated with the concept of a gay community) are merged with the sacred aspects of African American performance style, rendering the dance venue a "church for the children fallen from grace."[1]

Gay culture and black culture:
Double marginality, social affinity

The production and consumption of UDM is embedded in a cultural context whose history is specific to New York City. This history links UDM of the 1980s and 1990s to its precursor in the 1970s: disco. The roots of what in the late 1970s came to be known as the "disco craze" in turn lie in the meeting, merger, and overlap of two cultures whose urban variants increasingly interacted in the wake of the civil rights movement:[2] African American expressive culture and gay culture. Together, music and dance have long served, and continue to serve, as one of the main catalysts in that ongoing encounter.

In this chapter I situate UDM culturally and historically. Historically, UDM is linked to house and disco music, as they share the same cultural context. Like disco and house, UDM is the musical result of the interaction and intertwining of elements of black and gay cultures. The mutual acculturation of African American and gay cultures, however, began decades before the disco craze and can be explained by the historic role of New York City as a center for the arts as well as for a sizable African American population.[3] Based on my field data and published sources, it seems that the history of a culture that contains both sensibilities—African American and gay—is a sizable, albeit often overlooked part of the overall social history of America in the twentieth century.[4] Not until the 1960s and 1970s, however, do both gay and African American segments of American society become sufficiently conscious, aware, and vocal on a collective level to allow for both their self-definition and their assimilation into other cultural territories, including the mainstream of American society.

While the roots of this cultural exchange lie probably in the Harlem Renaissance of the 1920s, it was rather limited in scope then. In the 1950s, rock and roll and its media (records, radio and television) helped spread African American cultural expressions into the mainstream, but did little in terms of gay culture at the time.[5] With the emergence of the discotheque as an urban institution of magnetic mass appeal in the mid-1970s, however, more Americans than ever before could witness the emerging gay community use African American music and dance as a vehicle for individual and collective self-affirmation—much as American teenagers had been embracing them in the preceding two decades.[6] This is not to diminish the role of the gay bars and bathhouses in New York and other cities, nor that of the gay organizations of both the pre- and post-Stonewall eras. These terrains, however, and their roles in American sociocultural history are by now rather well charted. The discotheque as an institution for the formation of a culturally imprinted collective identity has so far received comparatively little attention.

Historical links between African American and gay cultures

In this century, the contributions by gay and lesbian Americans of African descent to the arts are as important as the general lack of their acknowledgment in the public discourse. During the Harlem Renaissance, jazz and literature were two artistic arenas that thrived not in the least due to the input of gay African Americans (or as they were referred to then, people who were "in the life").[7] However, homophobia and racism have permeated even recent scholarship reclaiming the importance of that period. In particular, "the racism of white gays has meant that the contribution of black culture to the development of gay sensibility has been ignored, while the homophobia of black scholarship has made invisible the contribution of lesbians and gay men to black culture."[8]

Homophobia and racism were also very much part of the social context of the 1960s. As American society experienced a decade of unprecedented social change, issues of race and sexuality carried over into the following decades. In sociopolitical terms, the Gay Liberation Movement did not emerge until after the Stonewall Riots in 1969; by then, however, its strategies and conceptual approaches took into account the gains made during the preceding decade by other movements, primarily the civil rights movement. One of the most important reasons for the successes of both movements was public visibility. What the Freedom Rides, sit-ins and voter registration drives in the Southern states had accomplished for civil rights of African Americans, Stonewall did for gay liberation. It made gay people—their issues, their desire to control their own destiny, to cultivate their own culture—more visible to society at large.[9] It is not coincidental that discotheques appeared as a new type of social institution in the post-Stonewall period.

In his book *Culture Clash: The Making of Gay Sensibility*, Michael Bronski lists publishing houses, record companies, theater groups, community-based newspapers and magazines as important institutions in the process of making gay culture more visible to the American mainstream. He does not mention the bars, bathhouses, and discotheques that figure prominently in other accounts, both fictional[10] and autobiographical.[11] In these latter institutions, it appears that gay culture initially remained as secluded and invisible as it had been before. However, gay sensibility found its way into the mainstream eventually, and the discotheque, disco DJs, and their music played a significant role in the process: "Gay sensibility . . . has had a tremendous impact on many aspects of popular culture. . . . Disco crossed over to the mainstream from black and gay culture. Much of the music began with black singers and entertainers. Gay bars and discos popularized it, proved that it was profitable, which brought it into the mainstream."[12]

A further link between gay and black culture is neither primarily historical nor political, but essential to many marginal cultures or subcultural phenomena in the twentieth century: the shared tension between status quo and change, between a focus on, and an affirmation of, an outsider's status as distinctive mark on one hand, and a desire to affect change toward acceptability and/or assimilation on the other. In the United States, this dynamic has always fundamentally affected the politics of gay as well as black cultures, and may continue to do so as long as they are accorded positions on the margins of American society by the mainstream and its institutions, especially the media.[13] The marginality of ethnic minorities is thus subject to similar dynamics as the marginality of a sexual minority, although it has been argued that "there is still some resistance to accepting the notion of a group by the shared experience of an outlawed sexuality."[14] In other words, in mainstream America, in terms of distinction as well as assimilation, the gains and accomplishments by African Americans happened earlier, are greater in extent, and have found greater acceptance in comparison to the efforts of gays and lesbians so far. This point is eloquently summed up by Cooper:

Until homosexuality as an identity evolves beyond imitative variations on traditionally "male" or traditionally "female" behavior, it will not enjoy true status as a third gender. This is why the creative freedom provided by cultural laboratories like nightclubs is so important. The promise couched in art that emerges from gender-ambivalent situations is that humans are still in a progress of evolution, and the discovery of a wholly unique third gender could liberate an entire realm of human potential that has only been suggested up to now. Cryptoheterosexuality begins with an awareness that "straight" and "gay" as terminology may be as fundamentally deceptive and fascist as the words "black" and "white" have become. If African Americans hadn't completely invented ourselves in ways that consistently defy or confound the definitions forced on us by Anglo-European domination, no one would recognize us or respect us as an autonomous people. This is the challenge that faces what is now known as the gay community, and the many cultural institutions whose very existence depends on the infusion of a gay sensibility.[15]

In an environment reflecting an increasing fragmentation not only of the American record industry,[16] but of American society overall,[17] one of the prime social institutions for the emerging "gay community" became the discotheque.[18] In the following, I argue that discotheques were ideally suited to the needs of the emerging gay community, and that they played a significant role in shaping a new sociocultural platform: a public, yet safe forum for gays to assemble, mingle, and socialize on their own terms. The labeling of this new addition to American society (in political terms as the gay liberation movement or, in sociocultural terms, as gay community) coincides historically with the emergence of the specifically "gay" discotheque.

The discotheque and gay liberation

The first discos to open in New York were Le Club in 1960, followed by Arthur . . . in 1965. These were the earliest manifestations of the disco as upper-class watering holes where the rich could be seen in a colorful setting. This syndrome continued into the Seventies through Studio 54 and Xenon. Under these circumstances the music has to be considered secondary—a backdrop. However, it was not these clubs that sustained the new music, even with Studio [54]'s major impact and the great DJs who played there. Rather, it was the underground clubs which catered to Blacks, Latins, and gays.[19]

In New York, the emergence of the discotheque of the 1970s was the result of a fusion or overlap of three distinct types of social dance environments prevalent in the 1960s, all of which featured recorded music, with or without the presence of a DJ. One precursor was based on the European, originally French, discothèque. In Manhattan, this type was typified by exclusive establishments such as Le Club, Arthur, El Morocco, and Cheetah, all conceptually derived of or modeled on the Parisian type—which, according to Goldman, had been brought to Park Avenue in New York by disco madam Regine Zylberberg (see also chapter 2).[20] Goldman goes on to describe how the French concept of disco was initially embraced by, and then consciously styled and marketed for, small groups of connoisseurs.[21] The earliest label for this group to become associated with discotheques as exclusive sites was the jet set. The cosmopolitan aspect of jet-set life led to a diffusion of this type of discotheque from Paris to places such as London and New York, cities proximate in terms of either geography or language.

In New York, during the 1960s and into the 1970s, the character of discotheques gradually changed to accommodate, besides the jet set, various groups within urban America that differed significantly from the earlier disco patrons who frequented what Goldman refers to as "chi-chi clubs," "established in New York to exploit the tradition of the chic, exclusive and exotically decorated Parisian boîte."[22] As outlets of music that expressed a rapidly changing popular culture, New York's discotheques of the late 1960s and early 1970s absorbed many of the social changes that affected American society at large during that period. Chief among those changes, and important for the development of disco culture in the 1970s, was the formation of increasingly vocal segments of society that felt largely shut out from the processes of decision-making and power-brokering across the country, but especially in urban centers. The most important of these were the young, ethnic minorities, women, and gays—urbanites who felt, and/or had been, pushed to the margins of American society. The two other precursors to the 1970s disco were filled with patrons from this milieu. One type attracted a primarily straight clientele, the other was frequented by primarily gay patrons.

In New York, the heterosexual type of proto-disco was exemplified by places such as Electric Circus[23] and Zodiac where DJs like Bobby "DJ" Guttadaro played an eclectic repertoire of rock (for example, Led Zeppelin, Chicago), rhythm and blues (Rare Earth, Booker T. & the MGs, the

Supremes) and early forms of what is now marketed as world music (San-tana, Osibisa) to a crowd markedly younger and less affluent than the jet set. This audience included anti-establishment pre-Woodstock hippies, struggling poets, musicians, actors and other artists, and a mix of working-class Caucasians, with some African Americans and Latinos.

The third type of dance venue grew out of neighborhood clubs or bars, both legal and illegal enterprises for socializing young gay men and women. Often these establishments served ethnically defined sections of New York, such as Harlem or the Latino portions of the Upper West Side and the Lower East Side. There, to the sounds provided by a jukebox or a DJ, older men (sometimes in drag) often acted as initiators and at times protectors of younger gays into "the life." In the 1960s, examples of this type of establishment were the Tabletop, which moved several times from its original uptown location on Third Avenue, Bosco's on Fifth Avenue, or André's on Eighth Avenue, all in Harlem. Others were located on the Upper West Side, such as the Candlelight and Picadilly on Amsterdam Av-enue, and in Greenwich Village, including the Stonewall Inn and the Snake Pit. After 1966, due mainly to a change in city government, much of urban gay life emerged from the sociopolitical closet to become both public and legal.[24] Still, many gay bars continued to be subject to police raids through-out the 1960s. One of these raids, however, involving the Stonewall Inn on Christopher Street, turned into a battle between gays and police that ulti-mately became a turning point in the history of gay life in New York im-portant enough to be remembered as the "Stonewall Riots."

The degree to which the Stonewall Riots on 28 June 1969 acted as a cata-lyst to synthesize these types of dance venue into one is a point of ongoing dispute among historians. Still, despite much mythologizing in the gay press, many commentators agree that "after Stonewall, . . . many lesbians and gays began to see social dancing not simply as a pastime but also as a powerful means of building a sense of communal gay and lesbian iden-tity."[25] While there is no similar agreement on which was the first gay disco-theque in New York, the first meeting of gays held to discuss the "sudden new defiance that seemed afoot among many homosexuals in New York City" after Stonewall took place on 6 July 1969, at the Electric Circus, the psychedelic rock disco on St. Mark's Place in the East Village.[26] By the fall of 1969, and in the spring of 1971, the two important post-Stonewall organ-izations addressing gay issues in New York City (the Gay Liberation Front and the Gay Activist's Alliance, respectively) had started to hold gay dance parties in lower Manhattan on a regular basis. By June 1971, the Gay Activist's Alliance headquarters on Wooster Street in Soho—known as the Firehouse—had become "the most popular gay dance club in New York."[27]

Initially, the DJs playing records at these parties were not professionals; rather, they were often recruited from among the organizers.

That notions of gay identity, gay community, and a specifically gay agenda reverberated as long and strongly as they did throughout the 1970s is arguably due in large measure to Stonewall and its aftermath.[28] During the same period, New York discotheques became environments in which the marginalized of the urban area (including gays), with a increasingly heightened sense of their group status, converged. The purpose was as much as to escape from societal pressures for an evening, as to affirm and celebrate a type of otherness that hadn't had a collective outlet before.[29] Still, the collective idea frequently did not extend beyond the issue of sexual orientation. "The fact that disco originated in black gay clubs did not stop white entrepreneurs from instituting racist door policies at many gay clubs."[30] Jack Carroll, who was dancing at Sanctuary in 1971, at Flamingo in the mid-1970s, and at the Saint in 1984, has offered a succinct summary of how (during a period he calls "the longest party in human history") the disco phenomenon spread simultaneously with a growing sense of a local gay community. In the following, I have chosen to summarize rather than quote the relevant passages of his internet manuscript.

In 1973, black music with a strong heavy beat and a gospel-derived tone had almost totally eased out anything from the former decade among gay men. Songs had become longer than the old format, and stations like WBLS mixed these in without interruption for several songs in a row. As a result, many gay men began to make long tapes of mixed dance music on their cassette recorders at home, and started trading these tapes. In addition, the jukeboxes began to disappear from gay bars: no one wanted to listen to single records anymore. At a point somewhere between 1973 and 1975, it was clear that a new era was arriving in gay life and in pop culture. It was from the black subculture and the gay subculture that the dominant lifestyle of the next ten years was to come, from 1973 to the mid-1980s. By 1975, the lifestyle of gay men in New York focused on three things: disco, drugs, and sex. At this point, gay life in the city was assertive to the point of being aggressive and very public; it was beginning to set the tone of popular culture for all of the country, straight as well as gay. The most obvious characteristic of this lifestyle was its sound and its inescapable presence in any gay milieu—the disco sound. WBLS began a feature of commercial-less taped music mixed and taped by the DJ of some popular disco. The kickoff night was "brought to you from the Crisco Disco," known as one of the wildest, low-life discos in the city, notorious for the heavy open drug use and the raw sexual atmosphere. This was a clear acknowledgment that gay men were becoming the trendmakers in disco music and dance.[31]

A few other sources support the views of Anthony Thomas, who, an underground dancer and hobby DJ himself, pointed to the origins of disco specifically in underground gay black clubs of New York City.[32] His assertion that "although disco is most often associated with gay white men, the roots of the music actually go back to the small underground gay black clubs of New York,"[33] however, is somewhat tempered by the agreement among many popular music historians who locate the roots of the disco phenomenon at the intersection between dance clubs and gay sensibilities.[34]

Accordingly, underground discos were the offspring of dance parties at nightclubs, lofts, basements and bars, held by and for a segment of urban society that—by default or choice—identified itself as being on the margins of mainstream society. This segment consisted largely of gays, African Americans, Latinos, artists, and to some degree, straight and gay women many of whom were musicians, poets, or visual artists. In this context, music other than what was played on commercial radio was embraced by DJs and their audiences, with the DJ assuming the role of musical programmer. Tucker makes the connection between these forms of discotheque and the emergence of the DJ as artist/musician explicit:

These ... discos offered the disc jockey as a species of pop artist. Through skill, timing, and taste, the disc jockey used two turntables to segue between records with compatible beats—the idea was to build and build the tension of the music until it "peaked," provoking screams of pleasure from the sweaty, exhausted, second-winded revelers on the dance floor. When combined with an array of lights pulsing and strobing to the rhythm of the music, a disco set overseen by a master disc jockey could be a hypnotic, ecstatic experience.[35]

In this way, discotheques became "focal points, contained environments, with a common music, where people gather together to do whatever people do in places where they come together to dance and celebrate, to entertain and be entertained."[36] During the years of the Carter administration, this entertainment was attractive enough to move from underground to mainstream status. As disco fever, it became a mass phenomenon made in the USA.

The African American imprint: The discotheque as church

The importance of the church as the rockbed of African American culture and as an institution associated with continuity and high degrees of autonomy and safety is well known and documented. Providing an environment in which a stylistic stamp of African origin was put on a European tradition, "the first Black church is often referred to as the 'invisible institution'" where "the essential ingredient was the secrecy needed to maintain freedom of expression and freedom from punishment for unlaw-ful assembly."[37] In other words, the formation of the ancestor of the first Black church was a largely clandestine, underground enterprise, even be-yond the period during which the conversion of slaves to Christianity was a topic of controversy among slaveholders. Whereas the need for clandestine religious gatherings of people of African descent has changed since the times of slavery, there are to this day cultural spaces defined largely by and for African Americans that are as "invisible" to mainstream America as the Black church was in its early days. The invisibility of the dance under-ground in New York City is but one of several features shared with the style and structure of African American worship.

As with most church activities, most clubbing takes place on weekends. The similarities do not end there, however. There are a number of concep-tual links between the church and the underground dance club as institu-tions: both feature ritualized activities centered around music, dance, and worship, in which there are no set boundaries between secular and sacred domains.[38]

Underground! That's the way slaves had to learn about religion, how to read, how to escape and go about their business to freedom—underground! If it wasn't for the Underground Railroad, I don't know where a lot of folks would be today. So let's bring the whole world underground! So they can see what we see, they can feel what we feel. If people had to dance the way we dance and feel what we feel I think everybody would be able to get along.[39]

When Black people go out on Friday nights, or Saturday nights, they are celebrat-ing life and a release, and so the movement is a part of that. When Black people go to jook joints, or to Saturday night fish fries, you are walking sacred territory. There is a way the only way you know who you are sometimes has to do with what you can do when you go home from work, change clothes, get with your partner and dance all night long.[40]

We'll all turn black so who's to know;
as a matter of fact, color, creed, and breed must go
—the underground.[41]

In her book *Jookin': The Rise of Social Dance Formations in African-American Culture*," Katrina Hazzard-Gordon grants two pages to the dis-cussion of disco (in the book's postscript). There, disco is discussed in the context of an overall deterioration of "black core culture," rather than as an extension of it.[42] Accordingly, disco is "glittering, . . . highly commercial and youth-oriented," and is portrayed as a perverted form of African American dance environment, as it was "controlled by Euro-American domination."[43] I would like to offer a contrasting perspective that situates both the underground disco of the early 1970s as well as the later underground clubs of the 1980s and 1990s in the continuum of institutions for African American expressive culture, especially in terms of music and social dance. From this perspective, the setting of an underground dance club in New York City may be viewed as a modern-day adaptation of the jook joint of the rural South of earlier times.[44]

As exemplified by the quotes above, this view is based on the premise that the concept of underground is connected to a cultural continuum that has informed much of the social life of African Americans in the United States; as such, it has been essential to the evolution of African American expressive culture. In addition to a position of marginality, long ascribed by a societal mainstream and based on various forms of racism and segregation, the contemporary social dance arena for African-Americans has been embraced and adapted by gay men and women, who, for decades, have also been marginalized by that same mainstream based on the taboo of homosexuality.[45]

As outlined above, the idea of disco as church relates to the emergence of discotheques as "safe" gathering places for gay persons in New York City. Frankie Knuckles's reference to the gay disco as "a church for the children fallen from grace" underscores the continuing blend of sacred and secular elements that has characterized the evolution of music and dance in Black America.

From my particular end of it, it's like church. For me, it's definitely like church. Because, when you've got three thousand people in front of you, that's three thousand different personalities. And when those three thousand personalities become one personality, it's the most amazing thing. It's like that in church. You go to any church. I mean, if the church holds five hundred people, that's five hundred different personalities in one room. By the time the preacher gets everything going, or that choir gets everything going, at one particular [point], when things start peaking, that whole room becomes one, and that's the most amazing thing about it.[46]

What Knuckles describes is a process where spiritual unity is placed before individual personalities. Not only does he not conceptually distinguish the DJ's performance from those on the dance floor, he does not consider them performances in the first place. "The word 'ritual' seems more appropriate than 'performance,' [particularly] when the audience is committed rather than appreciative," writes Charles Keil in the context of blues, following Ralph Ellison.[47] Inside a dance venue, the committed audience is on the dance floor. The type of institution (blues joint, church, dance club) is less relevant than the dynamics between those "becoming one" in the ritual of sound and motion (bluesman–audience, priest/preacher[48]–congregation, DJ–dance floor). In the Black church as well as the underground dance club, the music can be described as "unity music. It unites the joy and

Although he is better known as one of the most influential vocalists of house music, Robert Owens here is working a guest spot at the Choice on the Lower East Side. Cradling a 'lolly pop' headphone, he's working two Technics SL-1200 turntables, a Urei 1620 mixer, and a three-way crossover unit. *Photo © Tina Paul, 1999.*

the sorrow, the love and the hate, the hope and the despair of Black people; . . . It shapes and defines Black being and creates cultural structures for Black expression. Black music is unifying because it confronts the individual with the truth of Black existence and affirms that Black being is possible only in a communal context."[49] These dynamics, referred to by Knuckles in the context of a dance club, were mentioned almost verbatim six years earlier in reference to the ritual of African American religious worship: "When the expectations of the Black congregation or audience are met, performer and audience merge; they become one. The personalized interpretation of a given gospel selection generates a sense of ethnic collectivity and spiritual unity."[50] As with the Black church where musical participation is available to everyone present, the underground club is a place where one can find

the freedom to practice in a natural way the fundamental cultural expressions of Blackness—to unashamedly celebrate and worship with music, rhythm, movement, and emotions. For people who are too often silent and restrained during the week, unable to respond naturally to derogatory comments made to them and about them, the church is an emotional and spiritual refuge. Come the Sabbath, it provides the place, opportunity, motivation, and encouragement to "talk back," to join forces in joyous communion, commemoration, and celebration with others; to let feelings flow freely; to find spiritual peace in emotional release and be renewed. Talking back, call-response, testifying, spirit-dancing, releasing, and replenishing— being unabashedly Black—were and are the mainstay of cultural communion in the traditional Black church.[51]

"You better work!" Celebrating a Christmas party in 1989 at Nell's are DJ/host Johnny Dynell and friends who salute and compliment club manager Nell Campbell's version of voguing. *Photo © Tina Paul, 1989.*

Concepts and concerns of self-affirmation through music thus inform the participation of African American and/or gay patrons of an underground dance club as much as they do in settings of African American worship. The programming strategy of a DJ is thus similar to the way a preacher is likely to proceed in a Black church. He "begins . . . with calm humility, then proceeds to build strategically, but sincerely, to an emotional peak. At the climactic point of total spiritual immersion, the worshippers [and the dancers] are virtually compelled to respond."[52] In the context of African American expressive culture, the bluesman, the preacher, and the DJ have been and continue to be cultural heroes, figures who command respect and admiration from their respective followings as each is brought "under the sound of his voice."[53] And as was and is the case in the Black church and the underground discotheque or club, fundamental is "the opportunity for everyone present to participate in some meaningful way,"[54] to "demonstrate total mental, physical, and spiritual conviction," using "every means available—the hands, feet, and face—to convey the consuming force of the music."[55]

Not surprisingly, a further manifestation of the link between the sacred and secular in African American music is what Burnim and Maultsby refer to as the "gospel sound."[56] Since the 1940s, they note, it has "stimulated the growth and development of urban Black popular music." To this day, many artists and performers who have contributed to the repertoire of underground dance music served their musical apprenticeship in community church ensembles and choirs. Of course, this is true for older African American musical styles as well, and it is not surprising to see some of those styles and repertoires as part of the sound libraries of underground DJs. Soul and disco recordings by artists such as Teddy Pendergrass, Eddie Kendricks, Patti Labelle, First Choice, MFSB, and Chaka Khan, released on labels such as Motown, Philadelphia International, Salsoul, or Atlantic, are subsumed under the term "classics" by underground DJs. Classics are considered extremely important by many underground DJs as they are central to the creation of a bond between them and their dancers. David DePino makes the following connection between classics and the rapport with his crowd at Tracks, a club on the lower West Side that closed in 1992:

I know almost everybody on that floor. Whether it's by face or by name, I know them. They know me. They come up throughout the night. If you stay in the booth from beginning to end, I'd say about 75% of the room comes up and says hello and one point or another. It's nice. People don't realize . . . but that's what earning a respect of a fan is. They love you. They learn to love over the years. The memories you have given them, the boyfriend or girlfriend they might have met one night while you were playing, and had a wonderful time to the music—you bring a memory to them. That's why people love classics. When they hear classics, they don't just love them 'cause they're such great songs; they love them for what section or moment of time in their lives that record meant something to them. . . . You will never see a room go as crazy or peak off a record as they do on classics.[57]

David Lozada, who spent many a night at Paradise Garage, concurs, describing the way Larry Levan used to hold church at his club:

On Sunday mornings at around 7:00 A.M., Larry would stop all the dancing by putting on Aretha Franklin singing "Mary Don't You Weep." We knew he was giving us church. But then he would take us from [a Black] church to his church! After Aretha was done with her song, he would serve us fiercely! And he didn't do this just once, but for several weeks.[58]

THE HOUSE / GOSPEL CONNECTION

The contemporary New York dance music subgenre known as the "Jersey style" or "jersey" is associated with church-trained African American singers such as CeCe Rogers, Adeva, Blaze, Simone, and Michael Watford. These performers and producers incorporate not only stylistic vocal features of gospel music, but also a variety of themes, sacred and secular, social and political, that have long been associated with the Black church tradition.[59] Two of the most prominent instruments in gospel, the organ and the acoustic piano, have become stylistically characteristic sounds on house music recordings from New Jersey, New York, and Detroit, following the example set by Marshall Jefferson in Chicago.[60] Also from Chicago hail

This DJ specialty retail store on East 3rd Street sells new and used 12-inch singles, albums, CDs, and DJ accessories. Featuring a sound system powerful enough to fill a dance club, it has become a meeting place for DJs citywide. *Photo by the author.*

house veteran Joe Smooth, who released an album under the title "Promised Land" in 1988, and the gospel-trained vocal trio Ten City, which recorded several albums combining elements of gospel, soul, Phillysound, house, and jersey in the late 1980s through the early 1990s.[61]

These recordings evidence the extent to which house music and by extension much UDM are organic extensions of the same musical evolution—shaped largely by people of African descent—that shaped the gospel tradition. Still, the connections are manifested most convincingly in a performance setting. In performance, "Black musical traditions embody . . . a liberating potential that allows one 'to free oneself for a greater indulgence in life,' and to 'find release from the rigid rules restricting self-expression.'"[62] Black expressive style in music is characterized by the "integration of song and dance, that is, synchronized movement to the music."[63]

In other words, the acoustic phenomenon of musical sound is not perceived as conceptually separate from the physical phenomenon of dancing. Rather, "like music, dance is a socializing force that teaches . . . about relationships, unity of mind and body, feelings and facts, symbols and images, communal harmony and personal individuality."[64] "Dance is a testament, in form and substance, to the sensibility, experience and sensuality of Black Americans. The movements are not designed merely to mark time to the music or keep the beat of the rhythm, but to collect and harmonize those forces that inspire the concrete definition of a given image or message—to express the communal objectives of the participants."[65] "This communal message, this 'spirit talk' says . . . in effect, 'Let it be,' 'Do your own thing,' 'Be yourself!' without fear of reprisal or judgment."[66] This communal objective became as important for gays in the process of cultural struggle as it has been for African Americans. While music and dance as the instruments in the pursuit of this communal objective are indispensable, the location can vary. For African Americans, it has long been a church; for gay men, a dance club.

Conclusion:
Underground dance music as a celebration of marginality

The majority of the music played by DJs at New York's underground dance clubs is identified as house music, which has its roots in the black gay scene of urban Chicago during the early and mid-1980s. The majority of those who identify themselves as participants in the New York dance underground are either minority (primarily black and/or Latino) or gay, or both. Disco music, house music, club music, underground dance music—all share the association with marginal groups in urban American society. The two most influential groups are gays and/or African Americans. In a continually evolving environment constructed on the simultaneity and synchronicity of music and dance, these two cultures have traded with each other and, to a lesser extent, with those of other marginal groups, such as women (both straight and gay), Latinos, and Asians. The result is a cultural style that is always in flux, while maintaining certain basic features of African American expressive culture in an environment aesthetically and collectively shaped by gay men.

Redefined as communities, African Americans share with gay persons two key aspects that permeate their lives, their identities, and their arts: collectivity and marginality.[67] The strength of tight social networks and sheer numbers is especially meaningful in both communities. UDM provides the ritual through which collectivity and marginality can be affirmed and celebrated. From an African American perspective, the disco can become like a church, the most powerful and significant institution in the black community, as it symbolizes individual and collective safety and hope for salvation. From a gay perspective, the collective experience of music and dance in the safe and uninhibited environment of a dance club potentially affirms the validity of a gay sensibility, a gay aesthetic, a collective identity, and a marginal social position with subversive and political potential all at once.

SEVEN

Outlook
Underground Dance Music beyond the 1990s

"Dance 2000."
—Larry Heard, Distance Records, 1997

To review: In New York City, underground dance culture is historically the result of an overlap of African American expressive culture and gay culture. In contrast to the mainstream, both cultures are characterized by a higher interest in music and dance, and the concept of "underground" applies to both as marginalized and, at times, even controversial entities in American society. How these shared traits combine in a clubbing environment to form the basis on which to affirm and celebrate gay and/or black identities through music and dance has been central to this study.

Of primary concern here has been the relationship between music as musical practice or behavior, on the one hand, and social and cultural marginality as an extramusical context, on the other. Hence, I have responded to a general lack of understanding of the connection between music and marginality, as enacted in this specific case by bearers of African American and/or gay cultures in the musical world centered around UDM. As such, this account needs to be followed by others that study music and marginality in different contexts.

A second concern has been the DJ as a musical figure with relatively recent prominence. Recognizing the slow response of the musical academy to his gradual rise in the hierarchy of various musical cultures, this study explores the DJ as protagonist in discotheques and dance clubs of the "dance capital of world," New York City, and to some extent, his various roles as innovator, performer, musician, artist, and authority figure, not only on a local, but on a national and global scale.

The role of New York City itself as musical center has been a related, third issue. Addressing the issue of UDM as a primary marker of a particular local musical culture whose influence is felt around the globe (as the example of the Paradise Garage under DJ Larry Levan has shown) this study has probed UDM's ties to New York City as a geography that is home to various unique urban enclaves in which music plays a vital, defining role.

This study is intended as a contribution to the history of social dance in the United States. Although I have identified the main cultural strand from which musical and dance forms have sprung as African American, the associated cultural context comes with a history that has yet to be fully documented. In contrast to other rather well-studied strains of African American music, such as jazz and blues, UDM—together with disco and house as closely related musical categories—topically still represents a white spot on the map of American music in this century. There is ample room for additional studies.

In the aftermath of the sociopolitical reconfigurations in America during the 1960s, the discotheque became one of the central institutions of urban gay culture. In the 1970s, New York City became not only the capital of disco, but a mecca for open homosexuality as well. Many of New York City's influential DJs, such as Grasso, Levan, and Knuckles) got their start in gay discotheques, and built their reputation on a largely gay following. Larry Levan's reign at the Paradise Garage, as well as Frankie Knuckles's rise to "Godfather of House" or Junior Vasquez's long-term association with the Sound Factory cannot be explained without considering the consistent support these DJs had and have in gay communities and/or those defined by ethnicity. As these communities have been adversely affected in the 1980s by the advent of AIDS, crack cocaine, and a general economic downturn, urban nightlife underwent a series of insalubrious changes. As a new generation of dancers reached clubbing age, it encountered a scenario that differed significantly from the experience of their older peers.

The diversity of dance music types in the 1980s represents not only a diversification of musical styles, but also a fragmentation of dance music performers, industries, and consumers. While this fragmentation is sometimes seen as contrasting with the relative uniformity of the disco style of the preceding decade, a perspective of this sort does not take into account the marginal status allotted to communities within the African diaspora that gave rise to such musical forms as jazz, rhythm and blues, gospel, soul, disco, funk, or reggae in the first place.

As with disco originally, UDM appeals mainly to a limited urban clientele of gays and ethnic minorities in their twenties and thirties. As with disco, the music is produced largely by professional DJs, and issued on 12-inch singles released by small independent record companies. The indie, the 12-inch vinyl record and the DJ are key to this culture, which is thus set apart from the usual practices of the record industry as dominated by the major labels, and their practices of production, marketing and consumption. Mass media such as television and radio play a very limited role. The central form of exposure and consumption of the music is through dancing at a club, to a program of music conceived and actualized by a DJ.

As UDM's main musical styles, both disco and house originated in cultural sectors of urban America identified as either gay, black, Latino, or their combinations. Many years after the emergence of disco in New York, and of house in Chicago, the majority of those who identify themselves as participants of the New York dance underground are either minority (primarily black and/or Latino) or gay, or both. Disco music, house music, club music, underground dance music all continue to share the association with groups considered marginal to urban America. In a continually evolving environment constructed on the combination of music and dance, gays, Latinos and African Americans have blended their cultural vocabulary. Over time, UDM has provided the ritual through which group identity and marginality can be collectivity affirmed and celebrated in dance.

The primary musical instrument of the dance is the body. Bearer of multiple meanings in social, political, and sexual terms, the dancing body has the potential to become a most expressive as well as versatile instrument. As the carrier of a sexual identity, the dancing body has been particularly relevant to those who could not express their sexuality otherwise within modern Western society: homosexual men and women. In dance, the body is thus directly linked to the concept of marginality.

From the individual dancer's perspective, underground dancing is a personal, yet potentially collective response to musical sounds and signals shaped by a DJ. In relation to the DJ's efforts the dance becomes an interactive performance, and vice versa. The result is a simultaneous interaction between music, as sonic phenomenon, and dancing, as its physical correspondent. Affecting the interaction are music-immanent elements (explored in chapter 5) and nonmusical variables, the latter category including ethnicity, sexual orientation, age, and socioeconomic factors (such as AIDS and the recession of the late 1980s, as discussed in chapter 6).

UDM "comes to life" only in the interactive performance between DJ and dancers. This interaction is facilitated through a shared emphasis on aspects of musical rhythm, on a micro- as well as a macrolevel. On the microlevel of musical rhythm, DJ and dancers interact by maintaining a balance between constant features (pulse, meter, musical structure) and variable features (dynamics, sound, and repertoire). On the macrolevel of programming, the music may be organized in sets, or according to a particular style, tempo, or energy level. The DJ's interaction with the dance floor can be best maintained by means of the prioritization of micro- and macro-rhythms. In this way, the synchronization of the sonic and kinetic levels of UDM performance is generally aimed for, and, depending on the skill and knowledge of the DJ, achieved.

A second characteristic element of UDM has been described as collective performance. The concept of collective performance is central to any discussion of underground dancing. While the idea of performance applies equally to the DJ and the dancer, it is the simultaneous and synchronous multiplication of individual interpretations of the music across the dance floor that gives underground club dancing its specific collective character.

I placed the discussion of musical parameters, which, together with rhythm, shape the process of vibe creation and maintenance, in the framework of a larger context, a cultural dimension to which both the DJ and dancers relate. The cultural dynamics affecting UDM are paralleled by technological developments. Vinyl, after about forty years of market domination, is no longer the product of choice in the general recording industry. Rather, it has been marginalized to the extent that it has become the staple of a specialized industry that caters to the most loyal vinyl consumers: DJs and collectors who jokingly refer to themselves as "vinyl junkies." This industry is the dance music industry, and New York City is its center. In New York dance clubs, vinyl records continue to be the medium of choice among DJs. Throughout the 1990s, the indications have been that the vinyl market will continue to be central to the local dance music industry. Driven by the DJ's concern for the relationship between his performance and the reaction by the floor, spinning wax, at least for the time being, remains the basis for interactive musicking in the underground dance scene of the city.

The diminished role of vinyl in the recording industry is paralleled by a change in urban nightlife culture. The majority of my consultants perceive New York City nightlife as less dynamic compared to fifteen, ten, or even five years ago. This impression is corroborated by the fact that there are fewer underground clubs or after-hours venues in operation, and fewer people frequenting these remaining venues. Those who still do constitute a group of clubheads and hardcore dancers who avoid what they refer to as the "trendy" and "commercial" venues where the "tourists, posers, and B&T's" congregate. This core group, which most of my informants identify with, stands apart from a generation of so-called new schoolers, teenagers of the 1980s who have grown nearly to equal in number the older group, the "old school" of dancers. This distinction, however, is more frequently applied by the members of the older segment themselves who see the gradual displacement of one "generation" by another. Instead of a gradual "passing of the torch" (Burnett 1992, personal communication) from one generation of dancers to the next, there is little ideological overlap between the old and the new schools. The latter was weaned on visual media (especially music video); the former, on audio media. Their respective attitudes are made visible in different styles of language, dress, and dancing: communal, involving everybody on the floor (older generation) versus individualistic, with circles of nondancing spectators ("new schoolers").

There has also been a changing of the guard among club DJs. In contrast to veterans such as Levan and his peers, younger DJ are perceived to put less emphasis on individual style, "creative" programming, and on leading and "educating" a dance floor crowd. "DJs have become plain lazy," laments Stephanie Shepherd, a veteran of the New York dance music scene who launched its first trade paper, *Dance Music Report*.[1] Some clubgoers complain that club music now has a tendency to be more similar from one club to another, one DJ to another, one record to another. There's a perceived tendency toward a more homogeneous club sound, which is at times criticized as being bland and predictable. As many of the old-school DJs moved up to do better paid remix work for major label artists, a group of "new school" DJs took over in the clubs. This group grew up with a technology largely inaccessible to their predecessors: MIDI technology, digital recording, sampling, and automated mixing. During the 1980s, an almost complete shift of production techniques has occurred, from being song-oriented and with the use of performing musicians, to the "track" concept (on which the repertoires of many post-1985 indie labels such as Strictly Rhythm or Nervous are based). Accordingly, today's producers of underground dance music often dispense with song structure, traditional tonality—even with vocals altogether—and rely heavily on MIDI technology and computer-controlled instruments.

While important, the demographic and technological changes described so far do not fully account for the diminished vitality in the New York club scene of the 1990s. Rather, they are symptomatic of other processes of change that have simultaneously transformed the conditions of urban life in New York, and elsewhere. The impact of AIDS, and its effect on sexual behavior and leisure-time use by the nighttime public in general, but especially the traditional underground dance music patrons (artists, gays, and ethnic minorities) cannot be underestimated. That a temple of casual sex such as the Continental Baths, where Larry Levan got his start as a DJ in 1972, is unimaginable in a contemporary New York City says a lot about recent changes in attitude toward the body as the link between sex and music, and the seat of ever-dynamic identities.

There was a rather abrupt shift, around the mid-1980s, in the urban drug culture away from "recreational" drugs after the massive influx of crack cocaine introduced an unprecedented level of perceived and actual violence not only in the streets, but in the dance clubs as well. Because of the perceived and actual need for increased security provisions (weapon searches and metal detectors at the door), there was ultimately a deterioration of the "peaceful togetherness" image of the underground dance culture (note the first half of the name "Paradise Garage").

The revision, by city and community boards, of zoning and drinking laws applying to the nightclub industry, adversely impacted the number of clubs and of their hours of operation. A noticeable increase of enforced bureaucracy was seen citywide after a lethal fire at the Happy Land Social Club, an illegal social club for Latinos in the Bronx in 1990. The conservative elements in the city elected a mayor to give voice and support to their disapproval of nightlife culture in general (especially where marginal groups were involved); nonetheless, clubs such as Sound Factory, even Limelight, have continued to offer divergent definitions of leisure-time activities.

Finally, there is the commercial success of other dance music genres associated with underground industries (techno) as well as mainstream industries (hip-hop). While underground dance music is largely synonymous with house music, the increased popularity of techno and rave music in Europe and selected areas of the United States has contributed to the further marginalization of house, which, in contrast to disco and hip-hop, has yet to cross over to the mainstream popular culture. This marginalization has been exacerbated by the increased investment, by audiences and the recording industry alike, in hip-hop, a category of popular music that made the transition from underground to mainstream status in the mid-1980s. Since then, hip-hop has proven to be much more viable economically than house, to the extent that some struggling house labels have started to incorporate rap music. (For example, Strictly Rhythm, E-legal, and III East started their own rap subsidiaries, whereas NuGroove, dedicated exclusively to underground repertoire, folded in 1992.) To the extent that hip-hop and techno are genres embraced by and marketed at young (under twenty-five) black and white audiences, respectively, the potential of a progressive rejuvenation of the house market is comparatively diminished—notwithstanding the small overlap on the fringes between house and rap audiences, as well as between house and techno audiences (at least in New York City, especially Brooklyn).

Most recently, dance music of many guises has received a new marketing term: electronica. As an umbrella marketing term at once complementing and substituting for dance music, it has been able to find a slightly bigger market in the United States than it did four or five years earlier. "People are a bit more open to it now that it's called electronica. It makes me laugh because it's the same thing we've been having all these years. As soon as the media put a different name on it, all over a sudden it's okay. It's really a replay of what happened to disco," comments Roger Sanchez.[2] Michael Paoletta, currently dance music editor at *Billboard*, is more cautious:

House music is still ghettoized. We (in the U.S.) haven't reached a peak since the disco days. I admire what happened [with house-derived dance music] in Europe, but they never had to deal with the death of disco the way we did, which is unfortunate for this country. It really dirtied the word disco, even dance music. You'd think that it wouldn't matter after twenty years, because most of the people into dance music are in their twenties, but people are still afraid of dance music. It totally frustrates me. . . .

The scene has splintered into a number of small subscenes: the house scene is divided between straight [for example, Sound Factory] and gay [Roxy], and the gay scene is to an extent divided by color [Escuelita for Latinos, Warehouse for African Americans, Roxy for Caucasians]. There is a drum and bass scene, an electronic lounge scene, all with little or no overlap. And then there are those who are into drugs and who are not. What you heard at Twilo during the Gay Pride '99 party was most probably music for a crowd high on Special K. This fracturing began in the early 1990s, after Red Zone had closed, and places like Webster Hall began to open. Clubs needed more DJs to play more than one style in different rooms, so they lowered the salaries. And this had a ripple effect across the city, to the extent that being a DJ is so trendy now it's no longer a job for many. Apart from a few established DJs who have some job security, many DJs are now in the ridiculous situation of being told by their bosses what to play. This has had a negative effect on the music you hear around the city. Within each scene, diversity is hard to come by.[3]

Still, the underground dance scene of New York continues to renew itself while recovering from the impact of AIDS. In the words of dance music historian Vince Aletti:

What remains is the music. It was the music that brought us together, music that kept us in touch, music that saw us through and, finally, out. Appropriately, the same music that shaped our lives soothed our deaths. At the close of another memorial, when the opening bars of [MFSB's] "Love is the Message" came out over the speakers, the room turned instantly into a club at four in the morning, everyone riding the wave of emotions—mourning and celebration all confused—let loose by the music. When music is your way of life—your blood, your air, your ground—it informs every moment, even the silent ones. . . . The music never stops. It helps us to remember, helps us to connect, helps us to go on. And on.

Thirty years after David Mancuso's Loft opened its doors to underground dancers, this study underscores the need for more contextual studies of the relationship between music and dance. I chose UDM as the object of inquiry because it highlights the connection between music and dance in and as musical performance in a culturally significant and technologically revolutionary way. If we hold that dance is integral to music as a cultural expression, then I believe we need to add the music-dance nexus to the general agenda of cultural studies, urban anthropology, ethnochoreology, ethnomusicology, and other related fields.

Appendix:
A selection of 100 UDM records

*

Artist	Title	Label	Year
10 Classic Disco Records			
Manu Dibango	"Soul Makossa"	Atlantic	1972
MFSB	"Love Is The Message"	Philadelphia International	1973
South Shore Commission	"Free Man"	Wand	1975
Donna Summer	"Love To Love You Baby"	Casablanca	1975
Diana Ross	"Love Hangover"	Motown	1976
Trammps	"Disco Inferno"	Atlantic	1976
Carl Bean	"I Was Born This Way"	Motown	1977
Roy Ayers	"Running away"	Polydor	1977
Gloria Gaynor	"I Will Survive"	Polydor	1978
Loleatta Holloway	"Love Sensation"	Salsoul	1980
10 Garage Records			
Instant Funk	"I Got My Mind Made Up"	Salsoul	1978
Chaka Khan	"Clouds"	Warner	1980

Artist	Title	Label	Year
ESG	"Moody"	99	1981
Taana Gardner	"Heartbeat"	West End	1982
Peech Boys	"Don't Make Me Wait"	West End	1982
D-Train	"Keep On"	Prelude	1982
Eddy Grant	"Time Warp"	Epic	1982
Gwen Guthrie	"Padlock"	Island	1983
Manuel Göttsching	"E2-E4"	Racket	1984
Man Friday	"Love Heartache"	Vinylmania	1986

10 Chicago House Records

Artist	Title	Label	Year
J.M. Silk	"Music Is The Key"	D.J. International	1985
Fingers Inc	"Mystery Of Love"	D.J. International	1986
Adonis	"No Way Back"	Trax	1986
Pleasure Control	"On The House"	Bright Star	1986
Xaviera Gold	"You Used To Hold Me"	Hot Mix	1987
The House Girl	"Bessie Smith"	House	1987
Master C&J	"Face It"	State Street	1987
Steve Poindexter	"Work That Motherfucker"	Muzique	1989
The Believers	"Who Dares To Believe In Me?"	Strictly Rhythm	1994
Chris Gray	"Very Moody EP"	Subwoofer	1996

10 Acid house records

Artist	Title	Label	Year
Mr. Fingers	"Washing Machine"	Trax	1985
Sleazy D	"I've Lost Control"	Warehouse	1986
Phuture	"Acid Trax"	Trax	1987
Maurice	"This Is Acid"	Vendetta/A&M	1987
Jolly Roger	"Acid Man"	Ten	1988
Tyree Cooper	"Acid Crash"	House	1989
Bang The Party	"Release Your Body"	Warriors Dance	1988
D-Mob	"We Call It Acieed"	ffrr	1988
Laurent X	"Machines"	House Nation	1989
Armando	"Downfall"	Warehouse	1989

10 Jersey/club records

Artist	Title	Label	Year
Blaze	"Can't Win For Losing"	Quark	1988
Jomanda	"Make My Body Rock"	Big Beat	1988
Adeva	"Respect"	Chrysalis	1988
Intense	"Mighty Love"	Ace Beat	1991
Urban Soul	"Alright"	Chrysalis	1991
Sabrina Johnston	"Peace (In The Valley)"	Atco	1991
Susan Clark	"Deeper"	111 East	1991
Michael Watford	"Holdin' On"	Big Beat	1992
Alexander Hope	"Saturdays"	Easy Street	1993
Funky People Presents	"The Blaze Tracks EP"	Funky People	1995

Artist	Title	Label	Year
10 New York underground tracks:			
Lil' Louis	"French Kiss"	Epic	1989
JoVonn	"Running"	Warner	1990
Underground Solution	"Love Dancing"	Strictly Rhythm	1990
Bobby Konders	"The Poem"	NuGroove	1990
Mission Control	"Outta Limits"	D.S.R.	1991
Gypsy Men	"Hear The Music"	E-legal	1992
The Shelter	"Gate-Ah"	Shelter	1992
Nuyorican Soul	"The Nervous Track"	Nervous	1993
Junior Vasquez	"X"	Tribal America	1994
Armand Van Helden	"Witch Doktor"	Strictly Rhythm	1994
10 Commercial house records			
Earth, Wind & Fire	"System Of Survival"	Columbia	1987
Madonna	"Vogue"	Sire/Warner	1989
Lisa Stansfield	"This Is The Right Time"	Arista	1989
C&C Music Factory	"Gonna Make You Sweat"	Columbia	1990
Black Box	"Ride on Time"	RCA	1990
CeCe Peniston	"Finally"	A&M	1991
Crystal Waters	"Makin' Happy"	Mercury	1991
Whitney Houston	"I'm Every Woman"	Arista	1993
Robin S.	"Show Me Love"	Big Beat	1993
Everthing But The Girl	"Missing"	ffrr	1995

10 Tribal house records

Candido	"Jingo"	Salsoul	1979
Tribal House	"Motherland"	Pow Wow	1990
Kraze	"Voodoo Sun"	Project X	1992
A.T.S. feat. Mr. Jay	"Baa.Daa.Laa"	UMM	1992
B-Tribe	"Fiesta Fatal"	Atlantic	1993
Lords of La Habana	"Aiko"	Kumba	1994
Circle Children	"Zulu"	Strictly Rhythm	1994
Kuyoe's Children	"The Tribal Recordings"	Nervous	1995
Submission	"Women Beat Their Men"	Velocity	1998
MAW presents	"A Tribute to Fela"	MAW	1999

10 Trance house records

D-Mob	"Trance Dance"	ffrr	1989
Moby	"Go!" (Remixes)	Instinct	1991
KLF	"Last Train To Trancentral"	Arista	1991
Jaydee	"Plastic Dreams"	R&S	1993
Jam & Spoon	"Stella"	R&S	1993
Lazonby	"Sacred Cycles"	Brainiak	1994
The Volunteers	"Sundown"	Eye Q	1994
Keoki	"Take It"	Mic Mac	1994
Signal Hill	"Release It"	Mainline	1994
Deep Dish presents Prana	"The Dream"	Tribal America	1994

Artist	Title	Label	Year
10 Hi-NRG records			
Donna Summer	"I Feel Love"	Casablanca	1977
Sylvester	"You Make Me Feel (Mighty Real)"	Fantasy	1978
Village People	"Macho Man"	Casablanca	1978
Frankie Goes To Hollywood	"Relax"	Island	1983
Miquel Brown	"So Many Men, So Little Time"	Record Shack	1983
Evelyn Thomas	"High Energy"	Record Shack	1984
Dead Or Alive	"You Spin Me Around"	Epic	1986
Erasure	"Chains Of Love"	Sire	1988
Abbacadabra	"Dancing Queen"	Almighty	1992
Weather Girls	"Can U Feel It"	EastWest	1993

Notes

Preface (p. ix)

1. Braunstein (1998, 55).

1. Introduction (pp. 4–17)

1. In spoken and written usage, "DJ" is as common as "disc jockey" is rare. In this text, I shall refer to a person who deejays as a DJ.

2. As discussed by Africanists such as Chernoff (1979) and Nketia (1974).

3. My use of the term "urban subculture" is compatible with Slobin's concept of "micromusic" (Slobin 1992). This intersects with the notions of music as ritual and fan communities as "urban tribes," as explored in studies of heavy metal in Barcelona (Martinez 1993) and of San Francisco's dance music scene between 1978 and 1988 (Diebold 1988). See also the introduction to Morgan (1979), entitled "The Gathering of the Tribes."

4. Straw (1990).

5. I use the term "scene" as distinguished from "community," following Straw (1991). In this regard, see also Hannerz (1970); Kruse (1993); Wicke (1985); Yu (1988).

6. Hip-hop is a subculture marked by music that has recently attracted sizable scholarly attention (e.g., Hager 1984, Rose 1994, Toop 1991). Discussions of other underground scenes centered around music tend to be found in the popular press (*Spin, Vibe, Village Voice* and so forth) and local fanzines.

7. Gay (1991).

8. See, for example, Fernando (1994), Rose (1994), Toop (1991).

9. Hebdige (1979).

10. Outside the United States, UDM has sizable followings in London, Manchester, Glasgow, Tokyo, Hamburg, and several cities in Italy and in the Benelux.

11. See Clarke et al. in Hall and Jefferson (1976, 9–74).

12. Hebdige (1979); see also Keil (1985).

13. Kruse (1995).

14. See, for example, Kruse (1995); Limón (1983); Manning (1973); Pacini (1989); Robinson (1991). Note that not one of these studies is written by an ethnomusicologist.

15. I borrow the notion of "core culture" from Gwaltney (1980). See also the work of Hazzard-Gordon (1983; 1990, 174).

16. I borrow the term from Small who uses *musicking* to describe the activity of "all those involved in any way in a musical performance" (1987, 50), including performing, composing, listening, and dancing.

17. Male pronouns will be used throughout this text in view of the fact that most DJs are male. See also chapter 3.

18. Examples are Fox (1970) and Nelson (1989).

19. See Blockson (1987) and Still (1968).

20. The anthology in question is entitled "Notes from the New Underground." One of its contributors, M. Preston Burns, defines underground as an environment shaped by individuals who oppose "any portion of established authority, whether for constructive reasons or not. . . . Any group with ideas to improve or destroy the established authority is a subversive element within that authority. With the added strength of numbers, these become the underground" (as quoted in Kornbluth 1968, 210).

21. Orlova (1991); Rauth (1982).

22. Burnim and Maultsby (1987).

23. Buhles (1977).

24. Nolan (1997).

25. Yu's introduction to the music played at the site of her research was with the term "underground music" (1988, 63). Norfleet (1997) has studied New York City's hip-hop underground.

26. See Sukenick (1987).

27. Look for relevant evidence in period songs by Sly & the Family Stone, James Brown, and Curtis Mayfield, particularly the latter's 1971 composition "Underground" (see chapter 6, note 41).

28. Frith (1981, 244).

29. Chin (1999); also Tucker (1986, 532).

30. See also Carroll (1994).

31. Tucker (1986).

32. For a definition of popular music styles such as rhythm and blues, soul, and new wave, see Hitchcock and Sadie (1986).

33. These companies are referred to as "indies" in the industry, as opposed to large recording conglomerates such as MCA, Warner, Atlantic, which, since the 1970s, have been referred to as "majors" (see Glossary).

34. "Mediated music" corresponds to Roesing's concept of "transmitted music." Both are based on technological mediation and communication, and, as such, represent a pervasive mode of modern everyday musicking (Roesing 1984).

35. From here on, "gay" is used as abbreviation for "gay or lesbian," unless otherwise indicated.

36. I borrow the term from Gay and Baber (1987).

37. Thomas (1989).

38. See Clarke (1976, 47); Keil and Keil (1992, 3); Salamone (1988); Turner (1969); Yu (1988).

39. The London club Ministry of Sound was modeled on New York's Paradise Garage.

40. Straw (1990).

41. New York City refers not only to the island of Manhattan where most underground dance venues are located. For the purposes of this study, I am considering the entire metropolitan area, which includes parts of New Jersey (particularly the Newark area) and sections of Long Island that are beyond the borough limits of Queens and Brooklyn.

42. Yu (1988, 63).

43. Breh (1982).

44. Grandin (1989).

45. See, for example, Grenier and Guilbault (1990); Hennion (1990); Hosokawa (1984); Keil (1984); Manuel (1993); Middleton (1990).

46. Hanna (1979a); Kaeppler (1991); Youngerman (1975).

47. Hanna (1979a).

48. Giurchescu and Torp (1991); Kaeppler (1991); Banes (1994, 50).

49. Christensen (1991); Wilson (1985).

50. Notable examples are Günther (1969); Hanna (1992); Nketia (1974, 206–17); Wilson (1985).

51. Fabian (1983).

2. Disco (pp. 21–28)

1. See, for example Emery (1971, 1988); Hazzard-Gordon (1983, 1990); Poschardt (1998); Primus (1972); Stearns and Stearns (1968); Youmans (1968).

2. Clark (1974, i).

3. See Stearns and Stearns (1968, 1–7).

4. Clark (1974, 80).

5. Hazzard-Gordon (1990) and Malone (1996) are two examples.

6. Creekmur and Doty (1995, 437–46).

7. Examples are Bradby (1991, 1992); Collin (1997); Evans (1989); Friedland (1983); Gotfrit (1991); Hadley (1993); Hughes (1993, 1994); Langlois (1992); Lyttle and Motagne (1992); Mooney (1980); Redhead (1997); Reynolds (1998); Rietveld (1998b); Ross (1994); Straw (1993); Thornton (1995); Walsh (1993).

8. Examples are Harper (1989); Nolan (1969); Passman (1971); Williams (1986).

9. Compare the discussions of disco by George (1988, 150–55), Smucker (1980); and Ward (1998, 424–29). See also Goldman (1978), Poschardt (1998), and Haden-Guest (1997).

10. In his liner notes to Rhino Records' *Disco Box* compilation, Brian Chin makes the connection explicit. "Can all things disco be considered underground?" he asks rhetorically, and goes on to answer, "Well, think of the social mores of the time—or even those of today. Any place where young gays, blacks and Latins congregate in a spirit of welcome creativity an empowerment would be, by its very definition, out of the mainstream" (Chin 1999).

11. This is one of two instances where I use the French spelling of the word. Because my discussion focuses primarily on American phenomena, I have omitted the grave accent elsewhere.

12. Clark (1974, 1–2).

13. Ibid, 21.

14. Emery (1988); Brown (1971); Dixon-Stowell (1988, 351); Kurath (1965, 35); Stearns and Stearns (1968, 11–17); Kealiinohomoku (1958); Lomax, Bartenieff, and Paulay (1968, 234).

15. Clark (1974, 90).

16. See Lomax, Bartenieff, and Paulay (1968); Günther (1969).

17. To Clark's credit, her work documents the continued, if not increased effect of this influence. She concludes: "Beginning with ragtime, there occurred a developing assimilation of African-derived musical and dance style into the general culture" (1974, i).

18. Joe (1980, 11).

19. Clark (1974, 89).

20. These are described in more detail in Clark (1974); Goldman (1978); and Hazzard-Gordon (1990).

21. Breh (1982,166).

22. Goldman (1978, 24); Hazzard-Gordon (1990, 112).

23. Hogan and Hudson (1998, 171).

24. See Goldman (1978); Joe (1980); Shannon (1985); Straw (1990).

25. Hogan and Hudson (1998, 171, 214).

26. Chin (1999).

27. For example, in 1974 the Hues Corporation's "Rock the Boat" sold 50,000 copies in New York City alone, due mainly to club exposure (Chin, 1999).

28. Chin (1999).

29. Joe (1980, 21).

30. Hogan and Hudson (1998, 171).

31. If anything, the popularity of both Studio 54 and *Saturday Night Fever* helped boost the increasing animosity toward disco, especially among straight white males. See Braunstein (1998, 58) and Carroll (1994).

32. As quoted in Haden-Guest (1997, 150). See also Braunstein (1998).

33. Chin (1999).

3. The Cult and Culture of the DJ (pp. 33–56)

1. The title of this chapter paraphrases the title of a DJ symposium held in 1994 at New York University. Its contents were subsequently published in the journal *Social Text*. See Ross (1995).

2. Barry Walters (1988) also borrowed this title for an insightful portrait of New York DJ David Morales, published in the *Village Voice*.

3. In New York City, based on my estimate, male DJs by far outnumber female DJs (by a ratio greater than 10:1). The various reasons for the general scarcity of female DJs are discussed in more detail by Owen (1997) who, in an informal internet survey, counted fewer than one hundred female DJs nationwide.

4. Keil (1984, 91).

5. Out of context, a mixer can be understood to be either a device used to mix several audio signals before they are sent to the audio amplifier, or the person who operates this device in the position of recording engineer, recording technician (Kealy 1979), or DJ (Harvey 1983). Unless specified, in this text a mixer refers to the device, not the person.

6. Miezitis (1980, x).

7. At present, a new generation of consumers of mediated music is growing up without the exposure to vinyl records as the standard sound carrier format. To this and future generations, the CD may eventually become the main association for "record."

8. Holden (1986).

9. Some UDM DJs, such as Jason Load or Ken Carpenter, still favor and/or own older models that are no longer commercially available, such as the Technics 1100 or the belt-drive Thorens TK 125.

10. As quoted in Paoletta (1991, 12–13).

11. As quoted in Harvey (1983).

12. DePino (1992).

13. As quoted in Cooper (1990, 91).

14. Shannon (1985, 234). See also Klasco and Michael (1992).

15. Miezitis (1980, xx).

16. Harvey (1983, 29).

17. As quoted by Michael Musto (1995).

18. As quoted in Leaphart (1991).

19. As quoted by Reynolds (1991), writing as "Andyboy."

20. Goldman (1978, 50, 115).

21. Indeed, 45s share with 78s the limited time for recorded sound of about four minutes per side. For a DJ, an additional detraction is that 45s are often made

from recycled vinyl (as opposed to "virgin" vinyl for LPs and 12-inch singles), which results in a overall lower sound quality.

22. Levan's tremendous influence on dancers and both fellow and later DJs is still the talk of the town (Downey 1999). His untimely passing in 1992 led to a flurry of obituaries acknowledging his unique contributions to dance music worldwide (Frith 1992; Goldstone 1992b; Pareles 1992; Toop 1992). Mancuso's Loft is on hiatus while Siano returned from retirement in 1997 to work in New York again.

23. This applies as well to British club culture which is much more mainstream than underground in character (Toynbee 1993, 293).

24. I am excluding the radio DJ from this discussion whose role as cultural hero has been discussed by Harper (1989), Nolan (1969), and Williams (1986).

25. Toop (1991).

26. Dery (1991).

27. In the original introductory editorial to Harvey's article in the magazine *Collusion*, his interview partners are summarily labeled "New York's top mixers and DJs." The reprint of the article in *DJ* magazine ten years later substitutes the introductory editorial with an update that basically paraphrases the content of the original, while omitting the use of the word "mixer": "Steven Harvey and Patricia Bates spoke with many of the DJ/producers at the helm of the sound of the city" (Harvey 1993, 4).

28. Some early versions of DJ sets used two separate amplification systems without a mixer.

29. Kealy (1979); see also Tankel (1990).

30. The emergence of this industry has been described by Straw (1991).

31. See Joe (1980, 63–64); Shannon (1985, 205).

32. See Shannon (1985, 203 et seq.); also Fikentscher (1991)

33. Goldman (1978, 131). DJ Nicky Siano confirmed this point in several interviews with me.

34. Shannon (1985, 205).

35. Ibid, 206.

36. Examples of this approach are C&C Music Factory, Masters at Work (both from New York City) and the production teams Blaze and Smack (both from New Jersey). The success of these teams was based on the collaboration of DJs and musicians-turned-producers/remixers, whose names read like a who's who in the UDM scene: David Cole, Robert Clivilles (C&C Music Factory), Kenny Gonzalez, Louie Vega (Masters at Work), Kevin Hedge, Josh Milan (Blaze), Michael Cameron, Rico Tyler (Smack).

37. In contemporary Jamaican dance music culture, a "DJ" is what in New York is a "rapper" or "MC" (master of ceremonies). The term for disc jockey in Jamaica is "selector." There are obvious links between Jamaican dub culture and early hip-hop culture in New York (Rose 1994; Toop 1991).

38. Yu, who equates instrumentals and dubs, also comments on the appeal of dub versions as played by Larry Levan at the Paradise Garage (1988, 72).

39. The following list of examples is a short selection: "1018 Mega Mix" of Nia Peeples's *High Time* (Mercury Records, 1988); "Last Night At Garage Version" of Sofonda C.'s *Say The Word* (Klub Records, 1988); "The Last Dance At The 'Dise Mix" of RuffNeck's *The Power—The Rhythm* (New York Underground Records, 1988); "Shelter Mix" of Ten City's *I Should Learn To Love You* (Atlantic Records, 1990); "Original Shelter Mix" of Michael Watford's *Holdin' On* (Big Beat Records, 1992); "Shelter Mix" of Cassio's *Never Thought I'd See You Again* (Easy Street Records, 1993; "Sound Factory 12" Mix" of Frankie Knuckles's *Whistle Song* (Virgin Records, 1991); "Sound Factory Mix" of Junior Vasquez's *X* (Tribal

America/I.R.S. Records, 1994); "Danny Tenaglia's Twilo Club Mix" of Cerrone's *Supernature* (Pure Records, 1996); "Zanzibar Mix" of Cultural Vibe's *Ma Foom Bey* (Easy Street Records, 1989); "Zanzibar Mix" of Lil Louis & The World's *Nyce & Slo* (Epic Records, 1990). Also note that with the exception of Zanzibar, located in Newark, New Jersey, all venues mentioned are located in Manhattan.

40. The records referring to these DJs-turned-remixers are: "Larry Levan 12" MegaMix" of Gwen Guthrie's *Outside in the Rain* (Polydor Records, 1986); "Shep Pettibone Mix" of Janet Jackson's *The Pleasure Principle* (A&M Records, 1986); "Hurley's Deep House Remix" of Ten City's *Superficial People* (Atlantic Records, 1990); "Masters At Work Dub" of Ten City's *Fantasy* (Columbia Records, 1994).

41. This is an incomplete list of styles, exemplified by the following mixes: "House Mix" of Earth, Wind & Fire's *Thinking Of You* (CBS Records, 1990); "House Mix" and "Hip Hop Mix" of David Bowie's *Fame 90* (a 1990 remix 12-inch of the 1975 original on EMI Records); "Big House Mix" of Alexander O'Neal's *All True Man* (Tabu/Epic Records, 1991); "Hurley's Deep House Remix" of Ten City's *Superficial People* (Atlantic Records, 1990); "Hip Hop Mix" of Living Color's *Love Rears Its Ugly Head* (Epic Records, 1990); "Techno Mix" of Jordy's *Dur Dur D'Etre Bébé* (Columbia Records, 1992); "Rave Mix" of Desiya's *Comin' On Strong* (Mute Records, 1991); "The Tribal Mix" of The Lab's *Mary Stomp Your Feet* (Cutting Records, 1993).

42. Tannenbaum (1992).

43. See Tannenbaum (1992); Flick (1991); Chin (1987); Pareles (1990a).

44. As quoted in Tannenbaum (1992).

45. This show, broadcast nationwide on cable TV beginning in 1989, gave national exposure to rap and helped establish the genre as a part of the mainstream music industry.

46. Tannenbaum (1992).

47. Ibid.

48. In 1999, at least seven New York–based record labels specializing in UDM are headed by DJs-turned-producers: Clairaudience Records (Ron Trent); Masters at Work Records (Louie Vega, Kenny Gonzalez); R-Senal Records (Roger Sanchez); Sexy Records (Danny Tenaglia); Spiritual Life Records (Joe Claussell); Subliminal Records (Erick Morillo); Wave Records (François Kevorkian).

49. Finkelstein (1991).

50. Cooper (1990); Flick (1990).

51. Some DJs, such as Nicky Siano, have begun to incorporate CD-R for performing purposes, too.

4. The Dancers (pp. 58–78)

1. Small (1987, 50).

2. While representing distinct minorities on disco dance floors, there are those dancers who bring tambourines or whistles to the club to accompany the DJ (Shepherd 1982, 23). There is also a subculture of fan dancers. These are gay men who use colorful fans and cloths as extensions of the dancing body. For a brief description and history of this understudied performance art, see Straube (1999, 48).

3. Frith (1981, 246); Harvey (1983, 29); Miezitis (1980, xx); Yu (1988, 54).

4. Hanna (1979b, 19).

5. Hanna (1988, xiii).

6. Hanna (1979a).

7. Hanna (1988).

8. Chambers (1985, 209–10).

9. Ibid, 17.

10. In cases where access to a dance venue is policed through memberships, I would speak of the dance floor as a semipublic arena.

11. Turner (1969).

12. Ibid.

13. For a discussion of participation in music and dance as ritual, see also Pareles (1990b).

14. See for example, Clark (1974); Chambers (1985, 1986); Gotfrit (1991).

15. Gotfrit (1991, 183)

16. Chambers (1986, 135).

17. Pareles (1990b).

18. Yu (1988).

19. Examples of song titles invoking the Garage experience are Jovonn's "Garage Shelter" (Nite Stuff Records, 1994); Cevin Fisher's "Like We Used To" (Maxi Records, 1996); Byron Stingily's "Back to Paradise" (Nervous Records, 1998). For mix titles referring to Paradise Garage, see Chapter 3, note 39. A post-Garage continuation of this phenomenon is exemplified by a 12-inch entitled "Body & Soul," a direct reference by producer Alex J. to the late-1990s' party most closely styled to emulate the Garage experience (Nervous Records, 1999).

20. As quoted in Toop (1988, 71).

21. On separate occasions, I witnessed two club hosts use this exact same phrase: Tony Tune hosting Club Savage in 1991, and Kevin Hedge hosting DJ Timmy Regisford's party Temple in 1996.

22. Flick (1995); Galtney (1995); Owen (1995). Sound Factory was subsequently reopened under the name Twilo, while the old name was transferred to a new venue on Forty-sixth Street.

23. I find this idea echoed in the writings of Christopher Small on the relationship between music and society, particularly when he speaks of the "vision of the potential society" (1996, 209).

24. The hustle is one of the last traditional couple dances surviving in the contemporary milieu of social dance. Partners are generally connected by at least one hand, and one dancer leads the other in a series of learned step and spin sequences.

25. Hip-hop and freestyle dancing are related to breakdancing, the choreographic element of early hip-hop culture that helped transform rivalries between male gangs from violent clashes into dance competitions (Hager 1984; Toop 1991). Characteristic are fast footwork and spins executed with feet, body, or head as only floor contact. Expressive movement of the arms is the exception, as are women dancers. Voguing, by contrast, generally emphasizes arms and hands over feet. With its origins in the uptown black gay and transvestite community, the dance consists of improvised sequences of poses inspired by fashion models found in magazines such as *Vogue*, and remains associated primarily with gay dancers (Suggs 1990).

26. These terms are used, often synonymously, to refer to a line dance. It involves a set of patterns of steps that, when repeated four times, returns the dancers to their original position. Each sequence involves a 90-degree turn, usually in clockwise motion. One of the songs most likely to prompt club dancers to group themselves into lines is Marcia Griffith's "Electric Boogie" (Mango Records, 1983).

27. Sommer (1992, 98).

28. Cooper (1994).

29. Some examples are LNR's "Work It To The Bone" (House Jam Records, 1987), Steve Poindexter's "Work That Motherfucker" (Two 04 Street Records, 1992), Jack and Jill's "Work It Girlfriend" (Strictly Rhythm Records, 1992), Ru Paul's "Supermodel (You Better Work)" (Tommy Boy Records, 1992), and the "Workin' It Dub" by Masters at Work & Company's "Gonna Get Back To You" (Esquire Records, 1992).

30. As quoted by Sommer (1994, 7).

31. Miezitis (1980, xvii, xix).

32. On the relationship between divas and their gay fans and its interpretations, compare Braunstein (1998, 58), George (1988, 154), Boykin (1996, 217) and Ward (1998, 425).

33. The records Cooper alludes to have notorious status among underground DJs and dancers. Among them are Candy J.'s "Sweet Pussy Pauline" (Too Hot Records, 1989) and Karen Finley's "Tales Of Taboo" (Pow Wow Records, 1986). See also Crystal Balls' "Who You Callin' a Drag Queen?" (Strong Island Records, 1994). For a discussion of cryptoheterosexuality, see Cooper (1994, 58–59).

34. Gotfrit (1991, 186).

35. See Hanna (1988).

36. This description of underground clubbing is based primarily on fieldnotes from 1991 to 1992 and on personal experiences as a dancer in New York clubs, ranging from 1986 to 1999. In addition, there are a number of quotations from, and references to, writings on the subject from a dancer's perspective.

37. In the gay dance scene of Sydney, Australia, the same letters are used, albeit with a different translation. Accordingly, "B&T" stands for bus and train and is used to pejoratively describe outsiders to the scene (read: heterosexuals) and their main modes of transport to the inner-city dance parties (Lewis and Ross 1995, 32).

38. On his track "Make Me Dance" (NuGroove Records, 1991), DJ Basil "Hardhouse" Thomas (with help from engineer Ronald Burrell) pay homage to who's who in New York City's dance underground (on the "Hard For The DJ" mix). Mentioned among others are Frankie Knuckles and Larry Levan (the latter referred to as "the father,").

39. See Yu (1988); Toop (1988); Owen (1993). Yu's ethnographic study of the Paradise Garage is based on visits to, and encounters with, its patrons between 1984 and 1987. While limited in scope, this work is important not only because it is based on research done at the most influential underground dance venue in its time, but because it is one of the few accounts in which the dancers themselves speak on dancing in an environment they know as the underground. Yu, who accepted the invitation to become an underground dancer herself during her research period, understands ethnography as dialogue, and frequently lets her informants speak for themselves.

40. More than ten years after the closing of Paradise Garage, some established New York club DJs are said to "occasionally . . . out-garage each other" (Downey 1999, 43)

41. Galtney (1995).

42. As quoted by Flick (1995).

43. Goldstone (1992a).

44. As quoted in Joseph (1999, 129).

45. See Cooper et al. (1990); Davis and McCormick (1992); Goldstone (1992a); Marchese (1994); Miezitis (1980).

46. When Limelight reopened in 1999 after a hiatus related to charges of tax evasion and drug peddling, the DJ booth had been moved below the VIP lounge, one flight of stairs above the main dance floor, improving the overall quality of the sound.

47. Miezitis (1980, xv).

48. As described by Yu (1988, 16–29).

49. Yu opts to hide the identity of the Paradise Garage behind the name "Warehouse," the name of the venue in Chicago where Frankie Knuckles and his dancers helped forge the concept of house music.

50. This quote is taken from Yu (1988, 49).

51. Yu (1988, 60).

52. Cooper (1990).

53. Owen (1995, 30), my emphasis.

54. Burnett (personal communication, 1992).

55. Goldman (1978, 116–17); Lyttle and Montagne (1992); Owen (1995). See also Haden-Guest (1997); Collin (1997); Reynolds (1998).

56. Yu: (1988, 66).

57. The culturally specific aspects of this ritual will be discussed in chapter 6. For a discussion of the body in African American music, see McClary and Walser (1994).

58. "You played, indulging yourself, while remaining aware of choreographing your 'moves' to those around you to avoid trespassing and intruding on their playing. Only because everyone also played, and played to the same music, you were part of the crowd" (Yu, 1988, 62).

59. Hogan and Hudson (1998, 171).

60. Parrish (1999).

61. Fikentscher (1989).

62. Tucker (1986, 523).

63. Toop (1988).

64. Emery (1988, 365).

65. The transformations of house music in Europe are detailed in Collins (1997); Reynolds (1998); Rietveld (1998a; 1998b) and Veldhuis (1993). A particularly insightful insider's account is offered by Dave Haslam who deejayed at Manchester's Hacienda from 1988 to 1990 (in Redhead 1997, 168–80).

5. Underground Dancing (pp. 80–91)

1. John Blacking has suggested that "the musical [dance] styles current in a society will be best understood as expressions of cognitive processes that may be observed to operate in the formation of other structures. . . . Because music is humanly organized sound [and dance is humanly organized movement], there ought to be relationship between patterns of human organization and the patterns of sound [movement] produced as a result of human interaction" (as quoted in Youngerman 1975, 128).

2. Underground dancer Archie Burnett, as quoted in Sommer (1992).

3. Ibid.

4. In 1993, composer/producer Quincy Jones founded the monthly magazine *VIBE*, aimed primarily at young African Americans or Latinos and focused on music, film, fashion, and leisure.

5. DePino (1992).

6. Siano in turn learned from DJs David Rodriguez and Michael Capello, the latter of whom was tutored in deejaying by Francis Grasso. This suggest a continuously evolving oral tradition of deejaying in New York City, spanning from the pre-disco era into the 1990s.

7. As quoted in Harvey (1983).

8. Knuckles (1994).

9. "As you approach, even from a distance, you can already hear the faint beat, feel it reverberating ever so slightly in the pavement. It pulses like a heartbeat, growing with every step you take toward the disco entrance." (Miezitis, 1980 xvii).

10. As quoted by Sommer (1994, 7).

11. Yu (1988, 52).

12. Ibid, 73.

13. As quoted by Ressler (1994, 67)

14. Ibid.

15. Examples are The Untouchables' "Dance To The Rhythm" (Strictly Rhythm Records, 1991), M1-Then And Now's "Feel The Drums" (Emotive Records, 1992), Fingers Inc.'s "Can You Feel It" (Trax Records, 1987), The Tripp's "I Can Feel It" (Pow Wow Records, 1992), Darkman's "Annihilating Rhythm" (Strictly Rhythm, 1992), Illusion's "Annihilating Rhythm" (Guerilla/IRS Records, 1992), Chapter One's "Unleash The Groove" (Strictly Rhythm Records, 1991), and DV8's "This Beat Is Over" (Strictly Rhythm Records, 1991).

16. As quoted in Shannon (1985, 158).

17. Shannon (1985, 159)

18. Ressler (1994).

19. The record in question was an instrumental track, Djaimin's "Give You" (Strictly Rhythm Records, 1991).

20. Fikentscher (1991).

21. Harvey (1983).

22. Small (1987, 315).

6. The Underground as Cultural Context (pp. 93–107)

1. This is Frankie Knuckles's description of the Warehouse, the Chicago venue that gave birth to the concept of house music during his tenure there between 1976 and 1983 (Smith 1992). "Children" or "kids" are terms used by gay black men to refer to themselves (Hawkeswood 1996).

2. Bronski (1984, 87); see also Altman (1971, 185, 191–92)

3. See Watson (1995, 134 et seq.); also Bronski (1984, 76).

4. In addition to ethnographic data, I base this assessment on the following sources: Altman (1971); Boykin (1996); Bronski (1984); Carroll (1994); Chauncey (1994); Clendinen and Nagourney (1999); Creekmur and Doty (1995); D'Emilio (1983); Duberman (1993); Dynes (1987); Hawkeswood (1996); Hogan and Hudson (1998); Holleran (1978); Marcus (1992); Mayer (1973); Messerschmidt (1981); Miller (1995); Mizruchi (1983); Rutledge (1992); and Shiers (1988).

5. During the recording session for his hit "Tutti Frutti," Little Richard was forced to change the opening line of from "Tutti Frutti, Good Booty" to the less sexually explicit "Tutti Frutti, Oh Rooty."

6. See Carroll (1994). Of course, music and dance had been used in this manner by people of African descent for centuries.

7. Watson (1995, 134–37).

8. Bronski (1984, 76).

9. Ibid., 202.

10. See Holleran (1978) for a ficticious, yet documentary-like depiction of gay life in 1970s New York.

11. Carroll's account "Around Stonewall" is a brief autobiography ranging from the late 1950s through the 1980s (1994).

12. Bronski (1984, 181).

13. The relationship between marginality and culture in the context of black culture is discussed by Blauner (1970), Jeffries (1992), and Willhelm and Powell (1973). Compare with Chauncey's (1994) and D'Emilio's (1983) treatment of the same issue as pertaining to gay culture. See also Berry (1977), Mizruchi (1983), Kruse (1995) and Sanders (1990).

14. Bronski (1984, 6).

15. Cooper (1994, 58).

16. Straw (1990).

17. Tucker (1986, 504).

18. Hughes (1993); Carroll (1994).

19. Harvey (1983).

20. Goldman (1978, 26 et seq.); Joe (1980, 13).

21. Goldman (1978, 49).

22. Ibid., 44, 49.

23. Both Joe (1980, 20) and Sukenick (1987, 165–66) discuss the Electric Circus and its role as an early form of discotheque.

24. The Lindsay administration (1966–1974) provided significant relief to the city's gay population from his predecessor's Wagner repressive practices, the latter most visible in repeated purge campaigns directed against gay establishments (Carroll, 1994).

25. Hogan and Hudson (1998, 170).

26. Clendinen and Nagourney (1999, 25). A press release by the club's management advertising the night said: "We'll be open to the general public as usual, but we're especially encouraging gay people to come—and we really hope that everyone will dance together and dig one another" (ibid.)

27. Clendinen and Nagourney (1999, 76).

28. Ibid.; see also Hughes (1993).

29. While the Firehouse has been described as a progenitor of the huge gay discos of the mid-1970s, there was considerable disagreement within the Gay Activists Alliance on the issue whether dancing and gay liberation had anything to do with each other. After some heated discussions, the organization's constitution was rewritten to define the group as political *and* cultural, while its dances were built around political themes (Clendinen and Nagourney, 1999, 77–78, my emphasis).

30. Hogan and Hudson (1998, 171). In 1976, Paradise Garage recruited its initial membership in part from blacks who had been turned away from Flamingo, one of the popular gay discos in New York during the mid-1970s (Boykin 1996, 215) In the chronology section of the gay encyclopedia *Completely Queer*, editors Hogan and Hudson list one incident when members of the gay organization Black and White Men Together began holding weekly demonstrations outside the Ice Palace, another popular gay Manhattan disco, to protest the club's allegedly racist door policies (Hogan and Hudson, 1998, 655).

31. Carroll (1994).

32. "In the early 1970s, discos became a haven for a few groups who had been closed out of the increasingly white, sexist, male-dominated business that rock and roll was becoming. Gays, blacks, and women found in the discos a sympathetic environment" (Tucker 1986, 524). "Disco began in gay clubs. These were the first entertainment institutions of gay life. . . . The main business for early 1970s' discos were gays, blacks and Hispanics" (Joe 1980, 4, 20).

33. Thomas (1989).

34. Frith (1981, 128); Tucker (1986); Straw (1990, 122), Hughes (1993).

35. Tucker (1986, 524).

36. Miezitis 1980, xix–xx) here omits the reference to an environment initially shaped to fit specifically gay sensibilities. Steve Sukman, who managed the gay club Private Eyes on West Twenty-first Street in Manhattan, more tellingly distinguishes between the meanings of discos for gay and straight people: "Pleasure and being around your own people was the gay metaphor for disco; simple pleasure was its straight application" (as quoted in Braunstein 1998, 55).

37. Burnim and Maultsby (1987, 115–16).

38. This principle is eloquently described and documented in Murray (1976). A more recent example is Body & Soul, a weekly Sunday afternoon party in New York that carries on the tradition of Larry Levan's Paradise Garage. Accordingly, its three resident DJs, François Kevorkian, Danny Krivit, and Joaquin Claussell use their

"ersatz church" to create "a setting where people can lose themselves in music and use the music to get in touch with themselves as well" (Galtney 1999).

39. Gospel/house singer Michael Watford, as quoted in Flowers (1993, 7)

40. Bernice Johnson Reagon, in quoted in Grauer (1993).

41. This excerpt is from Curtis Mayfield's 1971 composition "Underground" (Curtom Records, 1972).

42. Hazzard-Gordon (1990, 174).

43. Ibid.

44. See Stearns and Stearns (1968, 5)

45. The experience of double prejudice, referred to as "double whammy" by many who are both gay and black (or gay and Latino) is eloquently discussed by Boykin (1996, 85–122). See also Ward for a discussion of the role of disco for "a section of black America which was doubly oppressed by virtue of race and sexual orientation" (Ward 1998, 424).

46. DJ Frankie Knuckles, as quoted in Leaphart (1991).

47. Keil (1966, 164); Ellison (1964, 257).

48. Following Keil (1966), underground deejaying is more "priestly" than artistic.

49. Cone (1972, 5).

50. Burnim (1985, 157).

51. Johnson, in Gay and Baber (1987, 316).

52. Burnim and Maultsby (1987 117; parentheses added).

53. Ibid.

54. Ibid, 116.

55. Ibid, 124; see also Levine (1977, 27–28, 189).

56. Burnim and Maultsby (1987).

57. DePino (1992).

58. Lozada (1999).

59. Examples are records such as CeCe Rogers' "Someday" (Atlantic Records, 1989), Adeva's cover version of soul/gospel singer Aretha Franklin's "Respect" (Chrysalis Records, 1988), Phase II's "Reachin'" (Movin' Records, 1988), Simone's "My Family Depends On Me" (Strictly Rhythm Records, 1991), and Michael Watford's "Holdin' On" (Atlantic Records, 1992) and "Michael's Prayer" (EastWest Records, 1994).

60. The gospel references in Marshall Jefferson's seminal "Move Your Body (The House Music Anthem)" (Trax Records, 1986) are echoed in Members of the House's "These Are My People" (Shockwave Records, 1991), Ebony Soul's "I Can Hardly Wait" (Eightball Records, 1992), Voices of 6th Avenue's "Call Him Up" (Ace Beat Records, 1992), Hula's "Praise" (Chicago Style Records, 1995), Moodymann's "Inspirations From a Small Black Church on the Eastside of Detroit" (KDJ Records, 1997), and Michelle Weeks's "Step Out On Faith" (Rambunctious Records, 1998). These records allude explicitly to the spiritual nature of soul and gospel music, by borrowing either stylistic traits, repertoire, or performers from these styles. Both "I Can Hardly Wait" and "These Are My People" feature samples from recordings by gospel artists BeBe and CeCe Winans; "Call Him Up" is a house arrangement of a gospel song with the same title by Rickey Grundy and Herman Netter, as is "Praise." Moodymann's "Inspirations From a Small Black Church on the Eastside of Detroit" is the treatment of a sampled and looped excerpt of a service inside an unidentified Sanctified church in Detroit, made possible through the courtesy of its pastor, the Reverend C. Brown.

61. Examples are songs such as "My Piece of Heaven," "Only Time Will Tell" (both EastWest Records, 1992) and "That's The Way Love Is" (Atlantic Records, 1989).

62. Garland (1969, 10), as quoted by Gay in Gay and Baber (1987).

63. Burnim and Maultsby (1987, 130); see also Levine (1977, 42–43).
64. Gay in Gay and Baber (1987, 13).
65. Ibid, 12–13.
66. Johnson (1987, 317).
67. Keith Boykin put this issue as follows: "Although blacks and gays are not the same, their movements are not the same, and even racism and homophobia are not the same, ultimately there is one shared experience that should unite blacks and gays: the members of both groups know what it means to be oppressed" (1996, 84).

7. Outlook (pp. 112–114)

1. Shepherd (1994).
2. Parrish (1999).
3. Paoletta (1999).

Glossary

A&R Abbreviation for artist and repertoire. In major record companies (*see* **major**), a department in charge of artist signings and artist development. In small independent labels (typical of the underground dance music industry), this task often falls to one or two persons who are recipients of many an unsolicited demo (*see* **demo**).

acapella One of several remix categories established in the early 1980s, consisting of the vocal track(s) of a 24-track master (*see* **master**), sometimes in addition to some percussion (*see* **percapella**). Used by DJs in combination with instrumental versions, often of another song.

bootleg (n., v.) In the recording industry, an illegally produced recording, without the consent of the author of the music or copyright holder. Sometimes the only form in which older, rare, or out-of-print material is available.

bpm Abbreviation for beats per minute. Measurement of musical tempo, as used by DJs.

break (n.) Part of a song that features a thinning of the musical texture, with strong emphasis on the rhythmic elements. Breaks are often chosen by DJs for mix with a second record or to peak a dance floor. Also referred to as *breakdown*.

breakbeat Music built around, or derived from, the breaks of R&B material (mostly pre-1985). Often a sped-up version of a hip-hop break (*see* **break**).

buzz The result of mouth-to-mouth advertising of a new song within a circle of industry insiders. The major objective of dance music promoters, a buzz is considered essential for any significant number of record sales.

CD-R Recordable compact disc.

classic (n.) Synonymous with *oldie*. A song of a bygone era, e.g., 1970s Philly-sound or disco. A song having found immediate and widespread acceptance by DJs and their audiences, irrespective of its commercial success in the top 100 or top 40 charts.

club 1. (n.) Establishment offering an indoor environment for social dancing, against an admission fee. May be legally licensed or illegal, may offer alcohol, may incorporate a membership list.

2. (v.) To go to a club, as in "to go clubbing."

3. (n.) Category of dance music; (*see* **club mix, club music**).

club mix The main remix category of mixes on 12-inch records, to designate a song's version geared specifically for dance floor applications.

club music Music produced for consumption at clubs. Often used synonymously with house music (*see* **house**).

clubhead Person with an above average dedication to clubbing (*see* **club**). Someone who frequents dance clubs regularly or frequently.

crossfader A device on a DJ mixer (rotary knob or slider) that controls the balance between two audio sources, such as turntables or CD players.

crossover 1. A shift of the sales base of a song or an artist, as a result of an appeal beyond the original audience, e.g., an underground song crossing over to a mainstream market, or a hip-hop remix of a pop song crossing over to a hip-hop audience.

2. An audio control device found in many DJ booths. It divides the frequency spectrum into bands that are then attenuated by control knobs. A three-way crossover will control the amount of bass, mid, and treble range sent to the corresponding amps and speakers.

Cut 1. (n.) Synonymous with *track* or *song*. A piece of music, encoded for visual identification by the turntable operator as a band of grooves of close proximity on a vinyl record. Each side may contain one or several cuts.

2. (v.) The opposite of *blend*. To switch from one song to the next in an abrupt fashion, usually by rapidly moving the crossfader on a mixer from one channel to the other.

Dancehall Jamaican club music. Began in the early 1980s with the displacement, in the production process, of studio musicians by cheaper studio technology (MIDI-controlled electronic keyboards, drum machines, sequencers). Pioneers of dancehall are Steely & Clivie and Gussie Clarke. Also known as *reggae dancehall*.

DAT Abbreviation for Digital Audio Tape. High-quality medium often used for mastering, developed in the 1980s.

Deep Serious, sincere, authentic, thorough. *Deep house*, a term used in the United States, is known as *soulful house* in the United Kingdom, and characterized by either a gospel-influenced vocal track, a minimalist instrumental arrangement, or both.

Demo Abbreviation for demonstration tape. Usually in cassette or DAT form, this is the draft stage for a piece of underground dance music, intended to draw responses from friends, DJs, and A&R personnel (*See also* **A&R, shopping**).

Disco 1. Category of 1970s dance music, derived from the abbreviation of discotheque as the main venue of consumption. Evolving from underground to mainstream status between the mid-1970s and 1978. Originally drawing from R&B, its commercialization increasingly involved European producers (e.g., Giorgio Moroder), leading to the subcategory eurodisco. Declined rapidly after an economic recession in 1979.

2. Abbreviation for discotheque, a venue for social dancing to mainly mediated music programmed by a DJ (*See* **club**).

disc jockey Also DJ or jock. Person in charge of programming, sequencing, and presenting prerecorded music, using 12-inch records, but at times involving other audio media, for social dancing at a club or discotheque. Key figure in the disco as well as underground dance music industries of the 1970s through the 1990s. Main consumer in the 12-inch single retail market after 1990.

DJ Abbreviation for disc jockey.

drag Cross-gender attire. May refer to men dressing as women, known as *drag queens*, or, vice versa, *drag kings*.

dub 1. (n.) One of several remix categories. Gives the remixer a high degree of flexibility, which usually results in doing away with song form, possibly with the vocal tracks as well. Is derived from DJ practices in Jamaica in the 1970s. May use a lot of studio effects such as echo and reverb. Sometimes used synonymously with *instrumental*.

2. (v.) To transfer audio from one medium to another, usually tape to tape (e.g., cassette, DAT, half-inch analog tape, one-inch analog tape).

edit (n., v.) The last stage of the remix process. Involves the splicing together—in analog or digital fashion—of segments of mixed song material (such as the *intro,* the *body,* the *break,* the *tag*).

EQ Abbreviation for equalizer, a device to decrease or increase certain points in the audio frequency spectrum. EQ-ing is usually a part of a mixdown session. In a DJ booth, EQ-ing is often accomplished with a crossover unit (*see* **crossover**).

eurodisco *see* **disco.**

fierce Supreme compliment, meaning intense. May apply to musical, visual, or personal qualities.

flavor *see* **groove, vibe.**

freestyle 1. Form of dancing, characterized by the absence of conventional step and body movement patterns. Instead, there is an emphasis on acrobatic and athletic foot and floor work that is often improvised.

2. Category of dance music aimed at the young Latino market. Combines elements of pop, rap, and electro (also known as *Latin Hip-hop*).

groove (n., v.) The feel, flavor, or vibe of a given piece of music, or the type of approach to it. Also used in nonmusical contexts, as in, "What he said didn't groove with me."

hardcore (adj., n.) Essential, elementary. Used in various contexts, to describe a no-frills quality or attitude, e.g., a hardcore clubhead or a hardcore sound. Also a style combining elements of punk, heavy metal, and techno music.

hi-NRG (also: high energy) A category of 1980s dance music geared toward a mainly white gay market. Used to describe non-R&B derived dance music, often by European artists or producers (*see also* **disco, eurodisco**).

hip-hop With and without hyphen, a term designated to an originally (late 1970s) Bronx-based youth subculture encompassing music (rap), dance (breakdancing), and visuals (graffiti, dress, and hairstyles). Pioneered the concept of the DJ as artist, the turntable as musical instrument. Crossed over from underground to mainstream status with the help of massive radio and television exposure in the mid-1980s. Is at present a multimillion dollar industry aimed at the under-21 generation. Sometimes synonymously used with *rap*.

hook Most memorable, catchy musical phrase of a song. May be vocal or instrumental. Often referential to, or identical with, the song's title.

house A style of dance music originating in gay black clubs in Chicago in the early 1980s. Its musical elements reflect the heritage of disco, while incorporating production techniques characteristic of the emerging home-studio industry, which helped DJs to become producers and artists. Falls into several subcategories such as *acid house, deep house, hip house, garage.* Often associated with DJ Frankie Knuckles, the "godfather of house" as a pioneer.

import A record made available on the domestic market by being imported, usually from Europe, by independent distributors and sold at a higher price per unit to the customer. Imports are rarer and more obscure than domestic releases and therefore highly desirable by many DJs.

indie Abbreviation for independent label. A record company working with a comparatively small budget, staff, and rather narrow repertoire. Sometimes enters relations with a major label to distribute its product. For the development of underground dance music in New York, indies such as Quark, Prelude, Salsoul and West End were important in the early 1980s. Later important indies include NuGroove, Big Beat, Strictly Rhythm, Cutting, E-legal, Easy Street, Freeze, Movin', Nervous, Eightball, King Street, Spiritual Life, Prescription.

intro Abbreviation for introduction, usually a layered, instrumental section that sets tempo and mood of a song. Is often extended for mixes on 12-inch records.

lay-over Playing two or more different audio sources simultaneously, e.g,. two instrumentals or one instrumental and a percapella (*see* **percappella**).

licensing Process of negotiation between two record companies, whereby one permits the other to release a record previously available only on the former to be released by the latter, usually in another geographic market, e.g., the United Kingdom or Europe. Can be a source of additional income for independent producers.

major Abbreviation for major label. A record company forming a part of the "Big Five" multinational corporate structures that dominate the recording industry worldwide (BMG, Matsushita, Polygram, Sony, Thorn/EMI, WEA). RCA, CBS, Mercury, Warner, Atlantic, and MCA are all majors.

master 1. (n.) The final stereo version of a song or mix, resulting from a mix session. Usually in high-quality analog or digital form.

2. (v.) Process of final EQ-ing (*see* **EQ**) of a record at a mastering plant, before the processes of plating and pressing.

MIDI Abbreviation for Musical Instrument Digital Interface, a system developed in the early 1980s by several major manufacturers that allows their product to communicate with one another. Allows one synthesizer to "talk" to another digital instrument, such as a sequencer, computer, or another synthesizer. A recording studio standard by the mid-1980s.

mix 1. (n.) The final balance of individually recorded audio tracks, as determined by a producer and executed by a DJ or by an audio engineer operating a mixing console. *see also* **remix**.

2. (v.) To treat and balance individually recorded audio tracks, creating a mix.

percapella A remix category derived from a contraction of acapella (*see* **acapella**) and percussion, i.e., a vocal track with additional percussion.

pressing The manufacturing of vinyl records, a process done at a pressing plant. 12-inch dance singles are known to vary widely in pressing quality.

promo Abbreviation of promotional copy. A limited edition pressing sent by the record company to chosen key institutions and persons in the dance industry (record pools, DJs), to promote new product. Sometimes features different mixes from the commercial 12-inch record released after the promo has helped create a buzz (*see* **buzz**).

pumping Supreme compliment referring to the quality of dance music as sound or performance, similar to slamming and working (*see* **working**).

R&B Abbreviation for Rhythm and Blues. Originally referring to commercial music made by and for African Americans in the 1950s, R&B is now used to refer to a broad commercial variety of African American musical styles, drawing on soul, doo-wop, disco, and urban contemporary.

record pool Organization for and by DJs who, for a membership fee, receive new product (12-inch singles) mostly from major labels. In return, pools collect feedback sheets from pool members and pass those on to the labels whose product has been given to DJs.

remix (n., v.) Reconstructive process applied to a finished master (*see* **master**) using two multitrack recorders. Often involving substantial re-recording (mostly of instrumental tracks, especially those of the rhythm section). The original vocal track is kept in most instances. To make a pop production appeal to a dance music audience (*see* **crossover**), a major label will hire a remixer/DJ to produce several mixes (*see* **remixer**).

remixer The person in charge of the production of several reconstructed versions of an already finished (and often commercially available) song. These versions often fall into established categories (e.g., club mix, dub, acapella, instrumental). A remixer is usually a recognized DJ hired by a major label.

spinning What DJs are hired to do, as in spinning records. Known in the United Kingdom as *deejaying*.

straight Heterosexual.

techno Category of 1980s uptempo dance music (usually faster than 125 bpm; *see* **bpm**). Originally associated with a house-derived style, pioneered in Detroit by DJs-turned-producers Derrick May, Juan Atkins, and Kevin Saunderson. At present techno is associated mainly with European product, with an emphasis on the nonacoustic, technological nature of synthesizers and studio technology. Embraced mainly by a young (under 25) and largely straight Caucasian audience.

track 1. Part of an audio recording dedicated to one audio source, e.g., vocals or piano. Usually configured in groups of 4, 8, 16, or 24 on a multichannel mixing console and multitrack recorder.

2. A piece of dance music, usually lacking vocals, and often songform structure. Since the mid- to late 1980s, in the dance underground, the track has replaced the song as predominant conceptual model for musical composition.

underground In the dance music industry, a term contrasted either with mainstream or commercial. Refers to a relatively small, geographically bounded, subcultural scene, with its own revered leaders (DJs), mechanisms of communication (language, clothing, dancing), and institutions (home studios, private or semiprivate clubs, independent record companies, specialty retail stores). Marked by a pride in cutting-edge ideology, and an insistence on separation from mass mediation via television, radio, or press.

vibe (n.) Often used synonymously with groove, flavor, feeling, atmosphere, to describe non-tangible qualities of a dance environment, pertaining to style, taste, or ambiance, as in "an underground vibe."

vogue A style of dancing, associated with gay men. Developed at gay social institutions such as drag balls, the dance is a free sequence of runway and fashion model poses as found in fashion magazines such as the French magazine of the same name.

wheels Hip-hop term for turntables, as in "Grandmaster Flash on the wheels of steel."

working 1. Supreme compliment, referring to musical qualities, as in "This break is working!"

2. Term to describe a DJ's extended creative treatment of a song, using at least two copies of the same 12-inch record simultaneously. Example: "Last night, Tony was working that record at Zanzibar."

3. Expressive way of dancing, often evoking encouragement from bystanders, who call out, "Work (it)!"

References 1
Text and Image

✵

Aletti, Vince. 1994. Liner notes. *The Project.* New York: Great Jones Records.

Altman, Dennis. 1971. *Homosexual: Oppression and Liberation.* New York: Dutton.

Banes, Sally. 1994. *Writing Dancing in the Age of Postmodernism.* Hanover, NH: Wesleyan University Press/University Press of New England.

Becker, Howard S. 1982. *Art Worlds.* Berkeley and Los Angeles: University of California Press.

Berry, Glenn A. 1992 "House Music's Development and the East-Coast Underground Scene." M.A. thesis, University of Wisconsin–Madison.

Berry, Jacqueline. 1977. "Black Jews: A Study of Status Malintegration and (Multi)Marginality." Ph.D. diss. Syracuse University.

Blauner, Robert. 1970. "Black Culture: Myth or Reality." In *Afro-American Anthropology: Contemporary Perspectives,* edited by Norman E. Whitten Jr. and John F. Szwed, 347–66. Foreword by Sidney W. Mintz. New York: Free Press.

Blockson, Charles. 1987. *The Underground Railroad.* New York: Prentice Hall.

Bradby, Barbara. 1991. "Do We Wanna Play House? Feminism, Postmodernism and the New Dance Music." Paper presented at the Sixth International Conference on Popular Music Studies, Berlin, Germany, 15–20 July.

———. 1992. "Sampling Sexuality: Gender, Technology and the Body in Dance Music." *Popular Music* 12, no. 2:155–76.

Braunstein, Peter. 1998. "The Last Days of Gay Disco. The Current Disco Revival Conceals Its Homo Soul." *Village Voice,* 30 June, 54–55, 58.

Breh, Karl. 1982. "High Fidelity, Stereophony, and the Mutation of Musical Communication." In *The Phonogram in Cultural Communication: Report on a Research Project Undertaken by Mediacult,* edited by K. Blaukopf, 165–77. New York: Springer Verlag.

Bronski, Michael. 1984. *Culture Clash: The Making of Gay Sensibility.* Boston: South End.

Brown, Greta Griffith. 1971. "Negro Dance in America: A Revelation." M.A. thesis, University of California, Los Angeles.

Boykin, Keith. 1996. *One More River To Cross: Black and Gay in America.* New York: Anchor Books.

Buhles, Guenter. 1977. "From Underground To Forefront. Carla Bley." *Jazz Podium* 25, no. 12:12–14; 26, no. 12:14–16.

Burnett, Archie. 1993. Interview by author, 14 November.

Burnim, Melonee V. 1985. "The Black Gospel Music Tradition: A Complex of Ideology, Aesthetic, and Behavior," in *More Than Dancing: Essays on Afro-American*

Music and Musicians, edited by Irene V. Jackson, 147–67. Westport, Conn.: Greenwood.

Burnim, Melonee and Portia Maultsby. 1987. "From Backwoods to City Streets: The Afro-American Musical Journey." In *Expressively Black: The Cultural Basis of Ethnic Identity,* edited by Geneva Gay and Willie L. Baber, 109–36, New York: Praeger.

Caldwell, Hansonia L. 1995. *African American Music: A Chronology, 1619–1995.* Los Angeles: Ikoro Communications.

Carroll, Jack. 1994. "Around Stonewall." web page. http://www.jessecc.com/index3/html.

Chambers, Iain. 1985. *Urban Rhythms: Pop Music and Popular Culture.* New York: St. Martin's.

———. 1986. *Popular Culture: The Metropolitan Experience.*Studies in Communication series. New York: Methuen.

Chauncey, George. 1994. *Gay New York: Gender, Urban Culture, and the Making of the Gay Male World, 1890–1940.* New York: Basic Books.

Chernoff, John Miller. 1979. *African Rhythm and African Sensibility: Aesthetics and Social Action in African Musical Idioms.* Chicago: University of Chicago Press.

Chin, Brian. 1987. "Remix Players Are Unsung Heroes." *Billboard,* 4 July, 58.

———. 1999. "In the Beat of the Night." Liner notes to *The Disco Box,* Rhino Records.

Christensen, Dieter. 1991. Editor's Preface to *Yearbook for Traditional Music* 23:ix–x.

Clendinen, Dudley, and Adam Nagourney. 1999. *Out For Good: The Struggle to Build a Gay Rights Movement in America.* New York: Simon and Schuster.

Clark, Sharon Leigh. 1967. "The Changing Scene in Social Dance." *Journal of Health, Physical Education, Recreation* 38:89–91.

———. 1974. "Rock Dance in the United States, 1960–1970: Its Origin, Forms and Patterns." Ph. D. diss., New York University.

Clarke, John, Stuart Hall, Tony Jefferson, and Brian Roberts. 1976. "Subcultures, Cultures and Class." In *Resistance Through Rituals: Youth Subcultures in Post-War Britain,* edited by Stuart Hall and Tony Jefferson, 9–74. London: Harper & Collins.

Collin, Matthew. 1997. *Altered State: The Story of Ecstasy Culture and Acid House.* New York: Serpent's Tail.

Cone, James. 1972. *The Spirituals and the Blues: An Interpretation.* New York: Seabury.

Cooper, Carol. 1990. "Life of the Party." *Egg,* June–July, 89–98.

———. 1994. "Check Yo'Self at the Door. Cryptoheterosexuality and the Black Music Underground." *Vibe* 2, no. 1: 54–59.

Cooper, Carol, Scott Currie, Montaug Haoui, Jill Selsman et al. 1990. "Clubs Made Easy." *Egg,* March, 53–60.

Creekmur, Corey K., and Alexander Doty, eds. 1995. *Out in Culture: Gay, Lesbian and Queer Essays on Popular Culture.* Durham: Duke University Press.

Cummings, Tony. 1975. *The Sound of Philadelphia.* London: Methuen.

Davis, Peter, and Maggie McCormick. 1992. "P.M. 'til dawn." *Paper,* June, 14.

D'Emilio, John. 1983. *Sexual Politics, Sexual Communities: The Making of a Homosexual Minority in the United States, 1940–1970.* Chicago: University of Chicago Press. (2d ed. 1998.)

DePino, David. 1992. Interview by author, 1 June.

Dery, Mark. 1991. "Now Turning the Tables . . . the DJ as Star." *New York Times,* 14 April.

Diebold, David. 1988. *Tribal Rites: San Francisco's Dance Music Phenomenon, 1978–1988.* Northridge, Calif.: Timewarp.

Dixon-Stowell, Barbara. 1988. "Popular Dance in the Twentieth Century," In *Black Dance from 1619 to Today,* edited by Lynne Fauley Emery, 339–66. 2d rev. ed. Princeton, N.J.: Princeton Book.

Downey, Austin. 1999. "Paradise Revisited." *HX Magazine* 408, 2 July, 43–44.

Duberman, Martin B. 1993. *Stonewall.* New York: Dutton.

Dynes, Wayne R. 1987. *Homosexuality. A Research Guide.* New York: Garland.

Ellison, Ralph. 1964. *Shadow and Act.* New York: Random House.

Emery, Lynne Fauley. 1971. "Black Dance in the United States, from 1619 to Today." Ph.D. diss. University of Southern California.

———. 1988. *Black Dance from 1619 to Today.* 2d rev. ed. Princeton, N.J.: Princeton Book.

Evans, Stephen T. 1989. "Nightclubbing: An Exploration After Dark." Paper presented at the BPS Scottish Branch Annual Conference, University of Strathclyde, Glasgow.

Fabian, Johannes. 1983. *Time and the Other: How Anthropology Makes Its Object.* New York: Columbia University Press.

Fernando Jr. S. H. 1994. *The New Beats, Exploring the Music, Culture, and Attitudes of Hip-Hop,* New York: Anchor Books.

Fikentscher, Kai. 1989. "Stylistic Pluralism in Contemporary Urban Dance Music." Paper presented at the Annual Meeting of the Mid-Atlantic Chapter of the Society for Ethnomusicology (MACSEM), Jersey City State College, New Jersey, 17–19 March.

———. 1991. "'Supremely Clubbed, Devastatingly Dubbed.' Some Observations on the Nature of 12-inch Dance Singles." *Tracking: Popular Music Studies* 4, no. 1: 9–15.

Finkelstein, Mark. 1991. Interview by the author, 16 December.

Flick, Larry. 1990. "As Majors Phase Out The 12-Inch, Dance Community Ponders An All-Digital Future." *Billboard* 102, no. 38:35.

———. 1991. "Remixers Have Found A New Beat. Major-Label Deals Offer Artistic Credibility." *Billboard* 103, no. 20:1 and 106.

———. 1995. "Junior Vasquez Sees Life After The Sound Factory." *Billboard* 107, no. 10:22.

Flowers, Kristopher. 1993. "Michael Watford." *Underground News* 13:7.

Fox, Hugh. 1970. *The Living Underground: A Critical Overview.* Troy, N.Y.: Whitston.

Friedland, LeeEllen. 1983. "Disco: Afro-American Vernacular Performance." *Dance Research Journal* 15, no. 2: 27–35.

Frith, Simon. 1981. *Sound Effects: Youth, Leisure, and the Politics of Rock 'n' Roll.* New York: Pantheon Books.

———. 1992. "Rockbeat: Larry Levan, 1954–1992." *Village Voice,* 17 November, 76.

Galtney, Smith. 1995. "Sound & the Fury." *Village Voice* 28 March, 30–31.

———. 1999. "Heavenly Bodies." *Time Out,* 29 July–5 August, 23.

Garland, Phyl. 1969. *The Sound of Soul.* Chicago: Regnery.

Gay, Geneva, and Willie L. Baber, eds. 1987. *Expressively Black: The Cultural Basis of Ethnic Identity.* New York: Praeger.

Gay, Leslie. 1991. "Commitment, Cohesion and Creative Process: A Study of New York City Rock Bands." Ph.D. diss., Columbia University.

George, Nelson. 1988. *The Death of Rhythm and Blues.* New York: Pantheon.

Giurchescu, Anca, and Lisbet Torp. 1991. "Theory and Methods in Dance Research: A European Approach to the Holistic Study of Dance." *Yearbook for Traditional Music* 23:1–11.

Goldman, Albert. 1978. *Disco*. New York: Hawthorn.

Goldstone, Adam. 1992a. "Clubthing! A Guide to Clubland N.Y.C." *Dance Music Report* 15, no. 11:8.

——. 1992b "Larry Levan, 1954–1992." *Streetsound*, November, 42.

Gotfrit, Leslie. 1991 "Women Dancing Back: Disruption and the Politics of Pleasure." In *Postmodernism, Feminism, and Cultural Politics: Redrawing Educational Boundaries,* edited by Henry A. Giroux, 174–95. Albany: State University of New York Press.

Grandin, Ingemar. 1989. *Music and Media in Local Life. Music Practise in a Newar Neighbourhood in Nepal.* Linkoeping, Sweden: Linkoeping University.

Grauer, Rhoda, executive producer, 1993. *Dancing*. PBS Television program. Chicago: Home Vision.

Grenier, Line, and Jocelyne Guilbault. 1990. "'Authority' Revisited: The 'Other' in Anthropology and Popular Music Studies." *Ethnomusicology* 34 no. 3:381–397.

Günther, Helmut. 1969. *Grundphänomene und Grundbegriffe des afrikanischen und afro-amerikanischen Tanzes*. Beiträge zur Jazzforschung/Studies in Jazz Research, vol. 1. Graz: Universal Edition. (In German).

Gwaltney, John L. 1980. *Drylongso: A Self-Portrait of Black America*. New York: Vintage.

Haden-Guest, Anthony. 1997. *The Last Party: Studio 54, Disco, and the Culture of the Night*. New York: Morrow.

Hadley, Daniel. 1993. "'Ride the Rhythm': Two Approaches to DJ Practise." *Journal of Popular Music Studies* 5:58–67.

Hager, Steven. 1984. *Hip Hop: The Illustrated History of Break Dancing, Rap Music, and Graffiti*. New York: St. Martin's.

Hall, Stuart and Tony Jefferson, eds. 1976. *Resistance Through Rituals: Youth Subcultures in Post-War Britain*. London: Harper and Collins.

Hanna, Judith Lynne. 1979a. "Movements Towards Understanding Humans through the Anthropology Study of Dance." *Current Anthropology* 20, no. 2:313–39.

——. 1979b. *To Dance Is Human: A Theory of Nonverbal Communication*. Austin: University of Texas Press.

——. 1988. *Dance, Sex and Gender: Signs of Identity, Dominance, Defiance, and Desire*. Chicago: University of Chicago Press.

——. 1992. "Dance," In *Ethnomusicology*, edited by Helen Myers, 315–26. 1st American ed. New York: Norton.

Hannerz, Ulf. 1970. *Soulside. Inquiries into Ghetto Culture and Community*. New York: Columbia University Press.

Harper, Laurie. 1989. *Don Sherwood: The Life and Times of "The World's Greatest Disc Jockey."* Rocklin, Calif.: Prima.

Harvey, Steven. 1983. "Behind The Groove. New York City's Disco Underground." *Collusion* 9:26–33.

——. 1993. "Behind The Groove." *DJ*, March, 4–9, 11–24.

Hawkeswood, William G. 1996. *One of the Children: Gay Black Men in Harlem*. Edited by Alex W. Costley. Berkeley and Los Angeles: University of California Press.

Hazzard-Gordon, Katrina. 1983. "Afro-American Core Culture Social Dance." *Dance Research Journal* 15, no. 2: 21–26.

——. 1990. *Jookin'. The Rise of Social Dance Formations in African-American Culture*. Philadelphia: Temple University Press.

Hebdige, Dick. 1979. *Subculture: The Meaning of Style*. London: Methuen.

Hennion, Antoine. 1990. "The Production of Success. An Antimusicology of the

Pop Song." In *On Record: Rock, Pop, and the Written Word,* edited by Simon Frith and Andrew Goodwin, 185–206. New York: Pantheon.

Hitchcock, H. Wiley, and Stanley Sadie, eds. 1986. *The New Grove Dictionary of American Music.* London: Macmillan.

Hogan, Steve and Lee Hudson. 1998. *Completely Queer. The Gay and Lesbian Encyclopedia.* New York: Henry Holt.

Holden, Stephen. 1986. "Disc jockey/Disco." In *The New Grove Dictionary of American Music,* edited by H. Wiley Hitchcock and Stanley Sadie, 626–27. London: Macmillan.

Holleran, Andrew. 1978. *Dancer From The Dance.* New York: Morrow.

Hosokawa, Shuhei. 1984. "The Walkman Effect." *Popular Music* 4:165–80.

Hughes, Walter. 1993. "Feeling Mighty Real. Disco as Discourse and Discipline." *Village Voice,* 20 July [Rock'n'Roll Quarterly], 7–11, 21.

———. 1994. "In the Empire of the Beat: Discipline and Disco." In *Microphone Fiends: Youth Music and Youth Culture,* edited by Andrew Ross and Tricia Rose, 147–57. New York: Routledge.

Jeffries, John. 1992. "Toward a Redefinition of the Urban: The Collision of Culture." In *Black Popular Culture,* edited by Gina Dent, 153–63. Seattle: Bay Press.

Joe, Radcliffe A. 1980. *This Business of Disco.* New York: Billboard Books.

Johnson, Carolyn. 1987. " Communion of Spirits." In *Expressively Black: The Cultural Basis of Ethnic Identity,* edited by Geneva Gay and Willie L. Baber, 293–320. New York: Praeger.

Jones, Alan, and Jussi Kantonen, 1999. *Saturday Night Forever: The Story of Disco.* Edinburgh and London: Mainstream Publishing.

Joseph, June. 1999. "On Wheels of Steel. André Collins Packs the Warehouse." *Paper* (June):129.

Kaeppler, Adrienne. 1991. "American Approaches to the Study of Dance." *Yearbook for Traditional Music* 23:11–22.

Kealiinohomoku, JoAnn Wheeler. 1958. "A Comparative Study of Dance as a Constellation of Motor Behaviors Among African and United States Negroes." M.A. thesis, Northwestern University.

Kealy, Edward R. 1979. "From Craft to Art. The Case of Sound Mixers and Popular Music." *Sociology of Work and Occupations* 6, no. 1:3–29.

Keil, Charles. 1966. *Urban Blues.* Chicago: University of Chicago Press.

———. 1984. "Music Mediated and Live in Japan." *Ethnomusicology* 28, no. 1:91–96.

———. 1985. "People's Music Comparatively: Style and Stereotype, Class and Hegemony." *Dialectical Anthropology* 10, nos. 1 and 2:119–30.

Keil, Charles, and Angeliki V. Keil. 1992. *Polka Happiness.* Philadelphia: Temple University Press.

Klasco, Mike, and Pamela Michael. 1992. "Crushing Grooves: The Art of Deejay Mixing." *Electronic Musician* 8, no. 10:58–65.

Knuckles, Frankie. 1994. Interview by author, 3 November.

Kornbluth, Jesse. 1968. *Notes from the New Underground: An Anthology.* New York: Viking.

Kruse, Holly. 1993. "Subcultural Identity in Alternative Music Culture." *Popular Music* 12, no. 1:33–42.

———. 1995. "Marginal Formations and the Production of Culture: The Case of College Music." Ph.D. diss., University of Illinois, Urbana-Champaign.

Kurath, Gertrude P. 1965. "African Influences on American Dance." in *Focus on Dance* 3:35–40.

Langlois, Tony. 1992. "'Can You Feel It?' DJs and House Music Culture in the U.K." *Popular Music* 11, no. 2:229–38.

Leaphart, Walter F., Jr., director. 1991. *What is House? An Insider's Look at Dance Music*. Television edit. Chicago: WMAQ-TV.

Levine, Lawrence W. 1977. *Black Culture and Black Consciousness. Afro-American Folk Thought from Slavery to Freedom*. New York: Oxford University Press.

Lewis, Lynette A., and Michael W. Ross. 1995. *A Select Body: The Gay Dance Party Subculture and the HIV/AIDS Pandemic*, London and New York: Cassell.

Limón, José. 1983. "Texas-Mexican Popular Music and Dancing. Some Notes on History and Symbolic Process." *Latin American Music Review* 4, no. 2: 229–46.

Livingston, Jennie, director. 1990. *Paris is Burning*. Documentary film. New York: Off White Productions.

Lomax, Alan, Irmgard Bartenieff and Forrestine Paulay. 1968. "Dance Style and Culture." In *Folk Song Style and Culture*, edited by Alan Lomax, 222–47. With contributions by the Cantometrics staff and with the editorial assistance of Edwin E. Erickson. Washington, D.C.: American Association for the Advancement of Science, Publication No. 88.

Lozada, David. 1999. Interview by author, 29 August.

Lyttle, Thomas, and Michael Montagne. 1992. "Drugs, Music, and Ideology: A Social Pharmacological Interpretation of the Acid House Movement." *The International Journal of the Addictions* 27, no. 10:1159–77.

Malone, Jacqui. 1996. *Steppin' on the Blues. The Visible Rhythms of African American Dance*. Champaign: University of Illinois Press.

Manning, Frank. 1973. *Black Clubs in Bermuda: Ethnography of a Play World*. Ithaca: Cornell University Press.

Manuel, Peter. 1993. *Cassette Culture: Popular Music and Technology in North India*. Chicago: University of Chicago Press.

Marchese, John. 1994. "The Mighty Nell's." *New York Times,* 27 February sect. 9:1, 8.

Marcus, Eric. 1992. *Making History: The Struggle for Gay and Lesbian Equal Rights, 1945–1990: An Oral History*. New York: HarperCollins.

Martinez, Silvia. 1993. "The Music of Barcelona's Urban Tribes." Paper presented at the Thirty-second World Conference of the International Council for Traditional Music (ICTM) Berlin, Germany, 16–22 June.

Mayer, Thomas F. 1973. "The Position and Progress of Black America." in *Modernization, Urbanization, and the Urban Crisis*. Edited by Gino Germani, 231–243. Boston: Little, Brown.

McClary, Susan, and Robert Walser. 1994. "Theorizing the Body in African-American Music." *Black Music Research Journal* 14, no. 1:75–84.

Messerschmidt, Donald, A. ed. 1981. *Anthropologists at Home in North America: Methods and Issues in the Study of One's Own Society*. New York: Cambridge University Press.

Meyers, Helen, ed. 1992–93. *Ethnomusicology*. 1st American ed. New York: Norton.

Middleton, Richard. 1990. *Studying Popular Music*. Philadelphia: Open University Press.

Miezitis, Vita. 1980. *Night Dancin'*. New York: Ballantine.

Miller, Neil. 1995. *Out of the Past: Gay and Lesbian History from 1869 to the Present*. New York: Vintage.

Mizruchi, Ephraim H. 1983. *Regulating Society: Marginality and Social Control in Historical Perspective*. New York: Free Press.

Mooney, Hugh. 1980. "Disco: A Style for the 1980s?" *Popular Music and Society* 7, no. 2:84–94.

Morgan, Roberta. 1979. *Disco*. New York: Bell.

Murray, Albert. 1976. *Stomping the Blues*. New York: McGraw-Hill.

Musto, Michael. 1995. "La Dolce Musto: The Sound Factory." *Village Voice*, 24 January, 12.

Nelson, Elizabeth. 1989. *The British Counter-Culture, 1966–73: A Study of the Underground Press*. New York: St. Martin's.

Nketia, J. H. Kwabena. 1974. *The Music of Africa*. New York: Norton.

Nolan, Tom. 1969. "Underground Radio." In *The Age of Rock: Sounds of the American Cultural Revolution*, compiled by Jonathan Eisen, 337–51. New York: Vintage.

Norfleet, Dawn. 1997. "Hip-hop Culture in New York City: The Role of Music Performance in Defining a Community." Ph.D. diss., Columbia University.

Orlova, Irina. 1991. "Notes from the Underground: The Emergence of Rock Music Culture." *Journal of Communication* 41:66–71.

Owen, Frank. 1993. "Paradise Lost." *Vibe* 1, no. 3:62–66.

———. 1995. "Sleepless in Manhattan." *Village Voice*, 28 March, 27–30.

———. 1997. "Spin Sisters. Women DJs Turn the Tables in Clubland." *Village Voice*, 2 December, 30–35.

Pacini Hernandez, Deborah. 1989. "Music of Marginality: Social Identity and Class in Dominican Bachata." Ph. D. diss., Cornell University.

Paoletta, Michael. 1991. "Tony Humphries. In the Mix." *Dance Music Report* 15, no. 5 (16–29 March):12, 46.

———. 1999. Interview by author, 17 August.

Pareles, Jon. 1990a. "If at First You Do Succeed, Remix and Remix Again." *New York Times*, 10 June, 26.

———. 1990b. "Paradise Found, at Least for a Moment." *New York Times*, 25 February, 26.

———. 1992. "Larry Levan, 38; His Tastes Shaped Dance-Club Music." *New York Times*, 11 November, D21.

Parrish, Troy. 1999. Interview by author, 16 August.

Passman, Arnold. 1971. *The Deejays*. New York: Macmillan.

Poschardt, Ulf. 1995. *DJ Culture*. Hamburg: Rogner und Bernhard. (In German.)

———. 1998. *DJ Culture*. London: Quartet.

Primus, Pearl. 1972. "Black America—Dance of the Spirit." *Focus On Dance* 6:20–22.

Rauth, Robert. 1982. "Back in the U.S.S.R.—Rock and Roll in the Soviet Union." *Popular Music and Society* 8, nos. 3 and 4:3–12.

Redhead, Steve, ed., 1997. *The Clubcultures Reader: Readings in Popular Culture Studies*. Oxford: Blackwell.

Ressler, Darren. 1994. "Sound Factory Automation." *EQ Magazine*, February, 67–68, 111.

Reynolds, Andy [writing as Andyboy]. 1991. "Frankie Knuckles: Beyond the Sound Factory." *Dance Music Report*, 14, no. 15 (17–30 August):4, 12.

Reynolds, Simon. 1998. *Generation Ecstasy: Into the World of Techno and Rave Culture*. New York: Little, Brown.

Rietveld, Hillegonda. 1998a. "Repetitive Beats: Free Parties and the Politics of Contemporary DiY Dance Culture in Britain." In *DiY Culture: Party and Protest in Nineties Britain*, edited by George McCay, 243–68. London: Verso.

———. 1998b. *This Is Our House: House Music, Cultural Spaces and Technologies*. Popular Cultural Studies 13. Aldershot: Ashgate.

Robinson, Deanna Campbell, et al. 1991. *Music at the Margins: Popular Music and Global Cultural Diversity*. Newbury Park, Calif.: Sage.

Roesing, Helmut. 1984. "Listening Behavior and Musical Preferences in the Age of 'Transmitted Music.'" *Popular Music* 4:119–50.

Rose, Tricia. 1994. *Black Noise: Rap Music and Black Culture in Contemporary America*. Hanover, NH: Wesleyan/University Press of New England.

Ross, Andrew. 1994. "Poverty Meets Performance. The Gangsta and the Diva." *The Nation*, 22–29 August, 191–93.

Ross, Andrew et. al. 1995. "The Cult of the DJ. A Symposium." *Social Text* 43:67–89.

Rutledge, Leigh W. 1992. *The Gay Decades: From Stonewall to the Present: The People and Events that Shaped Gay Lives*. New York: Plume.

Salamone, Frank A. 1988. "The Ritual of Jazz Performance." *Play & Culture* 1:85–104.

Sanchez, Roger. 1999. Interview by author, 5 July.

Sanders, Clinton R. ed. 1990. *Marginal Conventions: Popular Culture, Mass Media and Social Deviance*. Bowling Green: Bowling Green State University Press.

Shannon, Doug. 1985. *Off the Record*. 2d ed. Cleveland, Ohio: Pacesetter.

Shepherd, Stephanie. 1982. "A Retrospective of Disco." *Dance Music Report* 5, no. 11 (12–25 June):8, 10, 22–23.

———. 1994. Interview by author, 7 October.

Shiach, Morag. 1989. *Discourse on Popular Culture: Class, Gender and History in Cultural Analysis, 1730 to the Present*. Stanford: Stanford University Press.

Shiers, John. 1988. "One Step To Heaven?" In *Radical Records: Thrity Years of Lesbian and Gay History, 1957–1987*, edited by Bob Cant and Susan Hemmings, 232–47. New York: Routledge.

Simonelli, Victor. 1992. Interview by author, 7 November.

Slobin, Mark. 1992. "Micromusics of the West: A Comparative Approach." *Ethnomusicology* 34, no. 1:1–88.

Small, Christopher. 1987. *Music of the Common Tongue: Survival and Celebration in Afro-American Music*. New York: Riverrun.

———. 1996. *Music, Society, Education: An Examination of the Function of Music in Western, Eastern, and African Cultures, with Its Impact on Society and Its Use in Education*. Hanover, NH: Wesleyan University Press/University Press of New England. (Originally published 1977, New York: Schirmer.)

Smith, Richard. 1992. "The House that Frankie built." *Gay Times*, August, 36–38.

Smucker, Tom. 1980. "Disco." In *The Rolling Stone Illustrated History of Rock & Roll*, edited by Jim Miller, 425–34. New York: Random House/Rolling Stone Press.

Sommer, Sally. 1992. "The Hole in the Rug." *Village Voice*, 14 April 98–102.

———. 1994. "Check Your Body at the Door." *Dance Ink* 5, no. 4:6–11.

Stearns, Marshall and Jean Stearns. 1968. *Jazz Dance: The Story of American Vernacular Dance*. New York: Macmillan.

Stigwood, Robert, producer. 1977. *Saturday Night Fever*. Hollywood, Calif.: Paramount Pictures.

Still, William. 1968. *The Underground Railroad*. New York: Arno.

Straube, Trenton. 1999. "Fanning the Flames. The Ancient and Mystical Art of Fabric Throwing Unveiled." *HX Magazine* 408 (2 July):48–54.

Straw, William. 1990. "Popular Music as Cultural Commodity—The American Recorded Music Industries, 1976–1985." Ph.D. diss., McGill University.

———. 1991. "Systems of Articulation, Logics of Change: Communities and Scenes in Popular Music." *Cultural Studies* 5, no. 3:368–88.

———. 1993. "The Booth, The Floor and The Wall." *Public* 8:169–82.

Suggs, Donald. 1990. "Vogue Is? Willi Ninja Makes Life a Dance." *Village Voice*, 16 January, 36.

Sukenick, Ronald. 1987. *Down and In. Life in the Underground*. New York: Beech Tree.

Tannenbaum, Rob. 1992. "Remix, Rematch, Reprofit. Then Dance." *New York Times*, 30 August 30:23.

Tankel, Jonathan David. 1990. "The Practise of Recording Music: Remixing as Recording." *Journal of Communications* 40, no. 3:34–46.

Thomas, Anthony. 1989. "The House the Kids Built: The Gay Imprint on American Dance Music." *Out/Look* 5:24–33; reprinted in *Out in Culture: Gay, Lesbian, and Queer Essays on Popular Culture*, edited by Corey K. Creekmur and Alexander Doty, 437–46. London: Cassell; Durham: Duke University Press, 1995.

Thornton, Sarah. 1995. *Club Cultures. Music, Media and Subcultural Capital*. Cambridge: Polity Press. 1st American ed., Hanover: University Press of New England, 1996.

Toop, David, 1988. "Paradise Regained." *The Face*, February, 66–71.

——. 1991. *Rap Attack 2: African Rap to Global Hip Hop*. 2d ed., revised, expanded, and updated. New York: Serpent's Tail.

——. 1992. Untitled obituary for Larry Levan. *The Face*, January, 101.

Toynbee, Jason. 1993. "Policing Bohemia, Pinning up Grunge: the Music Press and Generic Change in British Pop and Rock." *Popular Music* 12, no. 3: 289–300.

Tucker, Ken. 1986. "The Seventies and Beyond." In *Rock of Ages. The Rolling Stone History of Rock & Roll*, edited by Ed Ward, Geoffrey Stokes, and Ken Tucker, 467–621. New York: Summit.

Turner, Victor W. 1969. *The Ritual Process: Structure and Anti-Structure*. New York: Aldine.

Veldhuis, Lydia. 1993. "Slave To The Rave. Plezierbeleving Binnen De Housecultuur." Master's thesis, University of Amsterdam. (In Dutch.)

Walsh, David. 1993. "'Saturday Night Fever': An Ethnography of Disco Dancing." In *Dance, Gender and Culture*, edited by Helen Thomas, 112–17. New York: St. Martin's.

Walters, Barry. 1988. "Last Night a DJ Saved My Life. David Morales Remakes Dance Music." *Village Voice* 7 June, 21–25, 34.

Ward, Brian. 1998. *Just My Soul Responding: Rhythm and Blues, Black Consciousness, and Race Relations*. Berkeley and Los Angeles: University of California Press.

Waterman, Richard. 1962. "The Role of Dance in Human Society." *Focus On Dance* 2:47–55.

Watson, Steven. 1995. *The Harlem Renaissance: Hub of African-American Culture, 1920–1930*. New York: Pantheon.

Weber, Max. 1991. *The Protestant Ethic and the Spirit of Capitalism*. Translated by Talcott Parsons. London: Harper and Collins.

Wicke, Peter. 1985. "Young People and Popular Music in the GDR: Focus on a Scene." *Communication Research* 12, no. 3:319–26.

Willhelm, Sidney M., and Elwin H. Powell. 1973. "Marginality: Black and White." In *Modernization, Urbanization, and the Urban Crisis*, edited by Gino Germani, 224–30. Boston; Little, Brown.

Williams, Gilbert. 1986. "The Black Disc Jockey as a Cultural Hero." *Popular Music and Society* 10, no. 3:79–90.

Wilson, Olly. 1985. "The Association of Movement and Music as a Manifestation of a Black Conceptual Approach to Music Making." In *More than Dancing: Essays on Afro-American Music and Musicians*, edited by Irene V. Jackson, 9–24. Westport, Conn.: Greenwood.

Youmans, John Greene. 1968. "A History of Recreational Social Dance in the United States." Ph.D. diss., University of Southern California.

Youngerman, Suzanne. 1975. "Method and Theory in Dance Research: An Anthropological Approach." *Yearbook of the International Council Folk Music Council* 7:116–33.

Yu, Arlene. 1988. "'I Was Born This Way': Celebrating Community in a Black Gay Disco." B.A. thesis, Radcliffe College.

References 2
Sound Recordings

*

Artist	Title	Label	Year
Adeva	"Respect"	Chrysalis	1988
Crystal Balls	"Who You Callin' a Drag Queen?"	Strong Island	1994
The Black Rascals	"The Definition of a Track"	New York Underground	1988
David Bowie	"Fame 90"	EMI	1990
Sofonda C.	"Say The Word"	Klub	1988
Candy J.	"Sweet Pussy Pauline"	Too Hot	1989
Cassio	"Never Thought I'd See You Again"	Easy Street	1993
Cerrone	"Supernature" (remix)	Pure	1996
Chapter One	"Unleash The Groove"	Strictly Rhythm	1991
Cultural Vibe	"Ma Foom Bey"	Easy Street	1989
Darkman	"Annihilating Rhythm"	Strictly Rhythm	1992
Desiya	"Comin' On Strong"	Mute	1991
D.H.S.	"The House of God"	Hangman	1991
D-Influence	"No Illusions"	EastWest	1992
Djaimin	"Give You"	Strictly Rhythm	1991
DV8	"This Beat Is Over"	Strictly Rhythm	1991
Earth	Wind & Fire	"Thinking Of You" Columbia	1990
Ebony Soul	"I Can Hardly Wait"	Eightball	1992

Artist	Title	Label	Year
Faithless	"God is a DJ"	Arista	1998
Fingers Inc.	"Can You Feel It"	Trax	1987
Karen Finley	"Tales Of Taboo"	Pow Wow	1986
First Choice	"Dr. Love"	Salsoul	1977
First Choice	"Let No Man Put Asunder"	Gold Mind	1977
Cevin Fisher	"Like We Used To"	Maxi	1996
Grampa	"She's Crazy"	Movin'	1993
Marcia Griffith	"Electric Boogie"	Mango	1983
Gwen Guthrie	"Outside in the Rain"	Polydor	1986
Basil Hardhouse	"Make Me Dance"	NuGroove	1991
Larry Heard	"Dance 2000"	Distance	1997
Hula	"Praise"	Chicago Style	1995
Illusion	"Annihilating Rhythm"	Guerilla/IRS	1992
Indeep	"Last Night A DJ Saved My Life"	Sound of New York	1983
Alex J	"Body & Soul"	Nervous	1999
Jack and Jill	"Work It Girlfriend"	Strictly Rhythm	1992
Janet Jackson	"The Pleasure Principle"	A&M	1986
Marshall Jefferson	"Move Your Body (The House Music Anthem)"	Trax	1986
Jordy	"Dur Dur D'Etre Bébé"	Columbia	1992
Jovonn	"Garage Shelter"	Nite Stuff	1994
Junior Vasquez	"X"	Tribal America	1994
Frankie Knuckles	"The Whistle Song"	Virgin	1991
The Lab	"Mary Stomp Your Feet"	Cutting	1993
Lil Louis & The World	"Nyce & Slo"	Epic	1990

Living Color	"Love Rears Its Ugly Head"	Epic	1990
LNR	"Work It To The Bone"	House Jam	1987
Master C & J	"Face It"	State Street	1987
Masters at Work & Company	"Gonna Get Back To You"	Esquire	1992
Curtis Mayfield	"Underground"	Curtom	1972
McFadden & Whitehead	"Ain't No Stoppin' Us Now"	Philadelphia International	1979
Mr-Then And Now	"Feel The Drums"	Emotive	1992
Members of the House	"These Are My People"	Shockwave	1991
Moodymann	"Inspirations From a Small Black Church on the Eastside of Detroit"	KDJ	1997
N.Y.C. Peech Boys	"Don't Make Me Wait"	West End	1982
Alexander O'Neal	"All True Man"	Tabu/Epic	1991
On The House feat. Marshall Jefferson	"Ride the Rhythm"	Trax	1986
Ru Paul	"Supermodel (You Better Work)"	Tommy Boy	1992
Nia Peeples	"High Time"	Mercury	1988
Phase II	"Reachin'"	Movin'	1988
Steve Poindexter	"Work That Motherfucker"	Muzique	1989
Professor Funk & The House Brothers	"Work Your Body Rap"	Underground	1986
CeCe Rogers	"Someday"	Atlantic	1989
RuffNeck	"The Power—The Rhythm"	N.Y. Underground	1988
The Chris Simmons Project	"Work It (Original Mix)"	Definitive	1993
Simone	"My Family Depends On Me"	Strictly Rhythm	1991
Joe Smooth	"Promised Land"	DJ International	1988
Byron Stingily	"Back to Paradise"	Nervous	1998
Ten City	"Fantasy"	Columbia	1994
Ten City	"I Should Learn To Love You"	Atlantic	1990
Ten City	"My Piece of Heaven"	EastWest	1992
Ten City	"Only Time Will Tell"	EastWest	1992

Artist	Title	Label	Year
Ten City	"Superficial People"	Atlantic	1990
Ten City	"That's The Way Love Is"	Atlantic	1989
The Tripp	"I Can Feel It"	Pow Wow	1992
The Untouchables	"Dance To The Rhythm"	Strictly Rhythm	1991
Various Artists	"The Disco Box"	Rhino	1999
Various Artists	"The Project"	Great Jones	1994
Voices of 6th Avenue	"Call Him Up"	Ace Beat	1992
Michael Watford	"Holdin' On"	Atlantic	1992
Michael Watford	"Michael's Prayer"	EastWest	1994
Michelle Weeks	"Step Out On Faith"	Rambunctious	1998

Index

Bold numbers refer to illustrations; n refers to an endnote.

Cole, David, 125n36
collective performance, 57–59, 60, 67, 76–77, 111
Collins, André, 72
Columbia Records, 43
communitas, 60–61
Cone, James, 102–103
Continentals Baths, 112
Cooper, Carol, 65, 96, 128nn, 33, 44, and 52
counterculture, 8, 9
Crisco Disco, 26, 99
cultural studies, xi, 114
Cutting Records, 55

Dahl, Steve, 11
dance, and the body as musical instrument, 59–61, 91; and the body as social instrument, 61–67; as ritual, 60–61, 75–76; definition of, 59–61; subversive potential of, 65–66, 75, 103, 107. See also social dance
dance music, definition of, 10–12
Dance Music Report, 17, 42, 112
Dash, Steve, 86
D'Aquisto, Steve, 84
Davis, John, 71
DeBenedictus, Michael, 90
DePino, David, 16, 39, 41, 72, 83, 85, 88, 91, 105
Dery, Mark, 44
Disco (book), 19
the disco concept, 22–23, 29, 34–35, 67, 97
the disco experience, 34, 58, 75
disco, literature on, 19–22
disco music, ix–x, 6, 9, 11, 12, 18, 20, 22, 25, 26, 28, 48, 78, 87, 89, 93, 94, 99, 100, 101, 106, 109, 110, 113, 114, 123nn9 and 10, 124n31, 131nn32 and 36, 132n45; African American imprint of, 23; backlash (The "Disco Sucks!" movement), 11, 18, 28, 124n31
discotheque, 12, 13, 23, 26, 64, 67, 73, 74, 77, 87, 94, 98, 99, 100, 102, 104, 107, 108, 109, 131nn23, 30, 32, and 38; emergence of the, 25, 77, 95, 96, 97
diva, 65, 128n32
DJ (disc jockey): as artist, 13, 28, 44, 100, 108; as the central musician in rap music, 44; club DJs, 3, 29, 33–36, 42, 48, 51, 77, 82; as cultural broker, 12; as cultural hero, 28, 44, 54; disco DJs, 43, 44; hip-hop DJs, 38, 39, 44; house DJs, 78; mobile DJs, 35–36; as new type of pop star,

26; as performer, 13, 33, 45–46; radio DJs, 35, 48, 125n24; reggae DJs, 78, 125n37; as soundscape architect, 8; techno DJs, 78; as "vinyl junkie," 13, 111
DJ Culture (book), 19
"Don't Make Me Wait" (song), 90
Doyle, Leslie, 53
"Dr. Love" (song), 89–90
drugs, ix, 7, 73, 74, 99, 113, 114, 128n46
dub mix, 51–52, 90, 125n38
Dynell, Johnny, 104

Easy Street Records, 55
El Morocco, 97
Elektra Records, 53
"Electric Boogie" (song), 127n26
Electric Circus, 97, 98, 131nn23 and 26
Electric Slide (social dance), 64
electro music, 78
electronica, reiterating disco, 113–114
E-legal Records, 113
Ellison, Ralph, 102
ethnochoreology, 16, 114. See also anthropology of dance
ethnography, xi, 17–18, 19, 21
ethnohistory, 17–18
ethnomusicology, xi, 4, 17, 19, 22, 34, 114
Escuelita (party), 114
eurodisco, 12, 78

"Face It" (song), 90
Fierstein, Al, 87
Finkelstein, Mark, 55–56
Finley, Karen, 66
The Firehouse, 98, 131n29
First Choice, 89, 91, 105
Flamingo, 99, 131n30
Fleming, Rochelle, 65, 90
Flick, Larry, 53
Flowers, Kristopher, 101, 132n39
flyers. See party flyers
For The Record, 45
Franklin, Aretha, 105
freestyle, 64, 78, 127n25

Gallery, 44
Galtney, Smith, 131n38
Garland, Phyl, 106
Gatien, Peter, 73
gay bars, 94, 95, 98, 99
Gay, Geneva, 106
Gay Liberation movement, 13, 95
"gay nights," 65, 67

ABOUT THE AUTHOR Kai Fikentscher holds degrees in jazz performance and composition from Berklee College of Music and Manhattan School of Music, as well as in ethnomusicology from Columbia University.

Library of Congress Cataloging-in-Publication Data

Fikentscher, Kai.

"You better work!" : underground dance music in New York City / Kai Fikentscher.

p. cm. — (Music/culture)

Includes bibliographical references and index.

ISBN 0–8195–6403–6 (hardcover : alk. paper) — ISBN 0–8195–6404–4 (pbk. : alk. paper)

1. Underground dance music—New York (State)—New York—History and criticism. I. Title. II. Series.

ML3540.5 F55 2000

781.5'54—dc21   00–009088